when the family hurts

J. BRUCE GRISI

when
the
family
hurts

Tyndale House Publishers, Inc., Wheaton, Illinois

All Scripture references, unless otherwise noted,
are from the King James Version of the Bible.
Other quotations are from the *New International
Version of the Bible* (NIV) © 1978 by New York
International Bible Society.

*Special thanks to Joan Milano for her help
in editing the rough draft of this book.*

First printing, February 1982
Library of Congress Catalog Card Number 81-52744
ISBN 0-8423-7996-7 paper
Copyright © 1982 by J. Bruce Grisi
Printed in the United States of America

To Linda,
    our children,
        and
    our larger families.

CONTENTS

PREFACE

I have long been aware of the pilgrim within me—the seeker who is moving toward that better place. Mine has been a search for understanding, an attempt to make some sense out of life. The search has been long, the acquisition of knowledge gradual, like the rising sun slowly turning the dark of night into daytime.

This book represents the place to which I have come. I do not see it as a journey's end but rather as an oasis, a place of coolness and refreshment. It is where I have been able to pause for a while and gain greater certainty that I am moving in the right direction.

The thoughts discussed here are a blending of the *contextual* approach to family therapy as developed by Ivan Boszormenyi-Nagy, M.D., and a theological approach to the Holy Bible which attempts to understand eternal truth in a contemporary setting. It is a focus on the place where the mental health clinic and the community called the Church intersect.

In my years of reading both within evangelical church literature and the literature of family therapy, I have been hard pressed to find a work that was not either too technically sophisticated for the layperson or too idealistic in approach. Some books do not recognize the brokenness already existing in people and in their relationships and the

difficult struggle necessary to realign family systems. Most
of the books I have read on Christianity and family seem
to be "how to" books that assume people are working
on virgin ground with brand new building materials. But
my experience is that we are in need of "urban renewal"
for families that have crumbled beneath extensive wear
and tear.

The families I have worked with, both in and out of the
Church, have been broken families. They have been, and
some still are, in crisis. They have needed, and some still
do need, remedies to heal wounds more than they have
needed measures to prevent wounds from occurring.

To those families everywhere that are still in the pain
of relational injury this message comes. It is a message
of hope. It is a message of encouragement. It is not an
attempt to offer the illusion of an instant cure-all. It is,
instead, an offer of some direction with which, after much
hard work, a family might experience healing and health.

INTRODUCTION

Although the details of specific family systems have been changed, this book is not fiction. These representations are of families I have come in contact with during my years involved with family therapy. You may see your family here. In fact, you may see your family reflected in several different family illustrations, since many of us share common experiences. We suspect that no one else can understand our problems because no one else goes through the kinds that we do. That simply is not the case. There is enough similarity within family systems to enable us to see characteristic areas of trouble. Exploitation of children by their parents, loyalty of a child to exonerate a parent by balancing shame with merit, or by siding with the shame by reproducing it in his own life, lack of societal trust stemming from lack of familial trust—these are all common situations in family life everywhere.

It must be understood that even though we can see common symptoms within different family units, we cannot treat each family exactly the same. Family systems, like individuals within a family, are unique. Each family is composed of different ingredients that are reacted to in different ways by the different personalities within the family. These individual reactions account for the difference between two families who have much background in common. So, a therapist cannot simply prescribe a solution for a family in crisis, but needs instead to walk with a family into the uniqueness of their system to find places where they might *reconnect* (reestablish healthy relationships). The therapist, however, cannot make these reconnections for a family. He must simply help them discover the areas of difficulty, and challenge the family with choices.

To make progress in our families takes tremendous courage—courage to admit the problems, courage to face other family members responsibly, courage to work through issues of unfairness and issues of shame, courage to change. This burden, though extremely heavy, becomes bearable when we realize that life charges hard prices no matter what choices we make, the hard prices of working out order, or the hard prices of living in our own form of chaos.

For several years I have had the opportunity to study under Dr. Ivan Boszormenyi-Nagy and Dr. Barbara Krasner in the Family Psychiatry Department of Eastern Pennsylvania Psychiatric Institute. To them I owe a debt for the deeper understanding of families and the therapeutic interventions that are conducive to ongoing growth. This understanding combined with my years of theological study and pastoral and social ministry elicited within me a sense of urgency in desiring to share this material with families everywhere.

ONE
RELATIONAL POVERTY
The Plight of the Family

As I looked into the face of the young man across from me, I could almost feel the hurt, confusion, and fear. In his twenty-seven years he had gone through enough suffering to last a lifetime. He had come to me seeking help, and he felt his need desperately.

Dave is the middle of three children, all boys. His parents are uneducated by today's standards, but it was the best their families were able to do for them. Dave's parents wanted more for their three boys, but their wish was not to be. When he was about twelve years of age, Dave began to notice that his father would come home from work and behave strangely. He would go to the bedroom he shared with his wife and stay there alone for hours. Periodically, his father would explode over nothing. Seeing a toy on the living room floor or finding no cream in the refrigerator for his coffee would send him into a rage. He would scream and yell for a long time. He would throw things around the house. Sometimes he would even go after the mother or one of the children to hit them.

Mother and the kids learned how to deal with the father, or at least they thought they did. Whenever she would see the eruptions coming, she would have the children put on their coats, and they would leave the house so that the father wouldn't hurt anyone. But things got worse rather than better. The father lost his job and finally was forced to seek professional help. He hadn't wanted to go to the mental health clinic, so he simply didn't cooperate with the program. When they put him on medication he would discontinue it himself. The family never knew what would happen next.

Finally, when the boys were older, their mother felt she could endure no more. She separated from her husband out of extensive pain, and even now, years later, cannot talk about their life together without tears. She still loves him, but because of his mental illness, she is not able to continue as his wife.

Dave was scarred. During the years when he should have been imitating his father for the shaping of his own manhood, he had to wrestle with the chaos in the home. Many of us cannot imagine what it feels like to live in terror in our own homes, to be afraid that at any moment our own father might lash out against us for some innocent gesture, or to plead with him for understanding and feel nothing but rejection in return. This is why Dave was scarred, and his brothers also show in their lives the marks of this troubled home.

Dave finds himself getting high on drugs a lot these days. Work is hard to cope with, his mind goes blank, and he trembles inside when someone raises his voice to him. In spite of his twenty-seven years, he has never had a meaningful relationship with a woman. He finds his "love" on the glossy pages of the magazines he buys from the adult book store.

"I need help," he said as he finished telling me about his most recent experience of booze, grass, and pornography. "I feel like I'm getting lost in life." Tears began to fill his eyes. "I don't want to be a lost person. I need help. Please help me."

Dave, according to statistics, is one of a multitude of young men and women who today find it increasingly difficult to make any sense out of life. They find life difficult because from their very foundations, from their childhood at home, family life didn't make any sense. Where does a person find trust if it cannot be found among those who are supposed to love him the most? Where can one find security if he cannot anchor to his own roots?

It is apparent that the family, as we have traditionally known it, is in trouble. Sociologists have speculated that at some point in the future the family, as a nuclear social unit, may be replaced by relationships contracted for a shorter period of time. Already we are seeing an increasing trend toward the dissolution of marriages and a reluctance on the part of the young to "make a commitment." We shouldn't be too hard on those who opt for living together instead of marriage when we realize the pain and hurt many of them have experienced as the children of broken marriages. Often at an age far below anything that would resemble emotional maturity, these children have been forced to choose to give their allegiance to one parent at the cost of being disloyal to the other. Even as adults, such a choice would tear us apart. What must it do to children, who are so very dependent on their parents? Certainly it must lodge deeply within their subconscious a real question about the safety of ever getting married themselves. Hence, to fulfill their need for companionship, intimacy, and love, they choose to leave space in the relationship to terminate if it doesn't go as planned.

Let us not get caught up into thinking that a broken or troubled family is necessarily one in which mother and father terminate their relationship as man and wife. Not at all. There are a variety of other forms of brokenness which one sees when sorting through family systems. Take Frank's home, for example.

Frank is an only child. From the day of his birth he was very special to both his parents. The problem is that his parents competed for his attention. Both were more interested in gaining first place in his life than in developing a relationship with each other. Frank early discovered that he could get whatever he wanted if he simply pitted one parent against the other. When one parent would say no, he would go to the other with tears and the sad sound of feeling unloved, and immediately parent number two would give him his heart's desire and prove his or her love to the child.

These parents were not malicious toward each other. They really did not see themselves struggling with one another over the boy; they each felt that they both loved the child and wanted the best for him. Gradually, however, Frank became their only basis for relating. Frank came to understand this not in the sophisticated terms of the psychologist or family therapist, but he knew he had a tremendous ability to make his parents happy or sad. He knew that he was often the cause of the arguing they did. He knew that he could cause one to "win" against the other by lending his weight. In this home too the child had to choose to be loyal to one parent at the cost of disloyalty to the other.

As a teenager, Frank started abusing drugs. This was his way of dealing with the turmoil of feeling helpless to love both his parents at once. This was his way of forcing his parents to start facing their need to work out their relationship together without him in the middle.

It worked, but only a little. When his parents discovered the drug problem, they pulled together to "help their son." They didn't pull together to help themselves; hence, they were treating the sneeze rather than the virus, the symptom rather than the cause. Frank seemed to recover, but the pressure of the family on him remained. He went away to college to "get out of the middle." His parents still did not relate to one another. They simply lived separate life-styles while living together. They didn't speak about their hurts, their fears, or their hopes until Frank came home from school. Then he was in the middle again.

As a result of the model of married life his parents presented to him, Frank today cannot hold together a relationship with a woman. His marriage in his early twenties ended in divorce. The other attempts he has made have likewise ended in failure. Beneath it all Frank knows that he hurt his parents' relationship and feels responsible to be with them to hold it together.

His parents also were part of the problem because they didn't work together at parenting but rather attempted to do so as individuals. The tragedy is that Frank is back on drugs and playing the role of the small child to two adults, who are still competing for his loyalty and favor. They all live together, but theirs is a broken home. Frank is not at all convinced that a marriage commitment is worth making or that there is anything beyond selfishness that motivates a couple to have children.

When families break down, we do not accomplish anything or solve any problems by attempting to pinpoint blame. At many different levels the entire family system has broken down. The parents have failed to hold children accountable; children have failed to call for responsible behavior from their parents; husbands and wives have failed to relate to one another fairly. So the system crumbles, and with the collapse of family units, our society as a whole is rocked. It becomes difficult to find stability anywhere. Why should today's generation expect to find relationships of permanence when they see none in existence?

Society itself feeds into this process of relational abandonment. It is not at all unusual today for the children of a given family to grow up and move thousands of miles away from home, each in a different direction. One lives in Los Angeles, another in Philadelphia, and still another in Florida. The parents live in Chicago, and get to see their children and grandchildren no more than once a year, if that. The moves have been made for something called "a career." The value of vocational success is balanced against the value of being close to one's family network. It's clearly a decision people make, and the weight of society is generally on the side of success rather than relationships.

It is common now for the average family to change homes once every five to seven years. Parents leave behind neighbors and friends. Children, moved from one school district to another, leave behind playmates and the teachers who serve them as adult models in life. Unlike the cultures of the past that placed heavy emphasis on people, ours has opted to emphasize things. Our basic question is no longer, "Who are you?" but rather, "What can you do?"

In this age of ever increasing mobility, older parents have become a problem to many of their adult children. The older folks do not take quickly to our notions of hopping from place to place. They do not want to leave for a destination miles away. They hit retirement age and no longer "do" anything. They are often considered social discards. In the rapid pace of our family life we have no time to slow down for them. By the millions, we have felt that they are best left in the care of homes for the aged.

Once, when I was attempting to share the gospel with an elderly man in one such home, I was stopped cold. I told him that God wants us to be his children and to love him as our father.

His response was quick and piercing. He said, "Love him like a son? I've been in here two years and my son never comes to see me. You mean to tell me my son loves me? Ha!" The breakdown in this family even reached into the gap between this man and his Creator. Again, faithfulness had lost. The question for many, both old and young, is, Why even marry and have a family if disappointment and heartbreak are so often the results?

It does, in fact, make a difference whether a person approaches his needs for love on the basis of marriage rather than just living together, but that isn't our concern at this point. With the deterioration of family systems, a person is not always given a basis to trust in them

enough to make these relationships seem worth the risk
of commitment. The abstract concept of faithfulness seems
to be eluding us today. If there is to be hope for us as
individuals in relationships with one another, we must go
back to the first of our relationships, the family, and seek a
reconnection. We must work out our relationships of family
loyalty which will give us the foundation to develop
relationships of loyalty within other spheres of life.

Those of us who believe in God and believe that he has
defined the parameters of life agree that God has not called
us to broken families. Understanding *sin* to mean "missing
the mark," we affirm that from the perspective of the plan
of God, broken families are a condition of sin. The
breaking had begun to take place even before Cain raised
the stone to destroy his brother.

In the plan of God, each child has two parents: his very
own father and mother. He is born as a product of their
love for one another. He is to be raised in the environment
of that love and to be given the strengths and wisdom of
each parent to cope with life when he reaches adulthood.
At some point he reaches out to find someone with whom
he might share his life and love, that together they in turn
might bear the fruit of their love and raise their children
to adulthood.

A dream? An unreachable ideal? In an ideal sense, it
is, because of the frailty of the human condition. But let
us not assume that we have to settle for discord and strife
as a way of life. Let us not assume that we cannot find
a reasonable harmony and a fulfilling love within the
marriage commitment. Even in our society of novelty
bombardment and rapid transience, there remains a
remnant who will affirm the joy of their marriages and
family lives. For them it has been worth the journey,
and they remain for us a reflection of what God planned
for us when he created a paradise for Adam and Eve.

TWO
THE FATHER'S SINS
The Effect on
Future Generations

Whether we accept the Bible as the Word of God or as a compilation of the wisdom of the ages, we cannot avoid the fact that it speaks to the way life is. In the early parts of the Bible, God says to Israel in the giving of the Law:

> *For I the Lord thy God am a jealous God, visiting the iniquity of the fathers upon the children unto the third and fourth generation of them that hate me.* Exodus 20:5, 6

Basically, we are to understand that the consequences of unrighteousness (not living rightly) carries over from one generation to the next. This often happens, even in cases where the child despises the behavior in his parent and swears he will never act in a similar way.

Steve is one of five children, three boys and two girls. Many times as a child he witnessed his father come home under the influence of alcohol and provoke a fight with his mother that ended in her getting physically beaten. His mother died in her late forties, a relatively early death. All of the children, including Steve, felt within themselves that their father had brought on her early death. Not only his physical abuse but his constant harassment had certainly so weakened her that when she became ill, her body was not able to fight off the infection and she eventually succumbed to it.

Steve remembers how bitterly he hated his father. He can recall feeling that if there were a God he should slay his father because he didn't deserve to live. Steve withdrew from the relationship with his father and dealt with him only out of the necessity that a child has to encounter a parent in day-to-day living.

In his mid teens, Steve left school and went to work. His dream was to get a place of his own—a place where he could get away from his father. He met Lucy around this time, and they began to make plans together. At eighteen he married her, and life seemed to be much better than it had been at home. Together they were able to earn enough to pay their rent, operate their automobile, and provide for all that they considered important in life.

Steve's father died shortly after he married Lucy. Steve went to the funeral services out of what he describes as a sense of responsibility. He felt no remorse, no sense of loss; he said he felt nothing at all. By this time he had so cut himself off from his father that nothing within him could respond to his death. He didn't even feel enough to be glad that this man, who had been the object of so much of his bitterness, was finally gone.

After four years of marriage, Lucy became pregnant. Both she and Steve had expressed a desire for children, but were not aware of all that having a family would entail. The first problem came when Lucy had to stop work. Until then, they had counted on her income as well as his to meet their monthly expenses. Suddenly, they were finding themselves never having enough money. They started to abuse their credit cards and then to make consolidation loans. This monster of borrowing was, of course, never fed; it simply kept crying for more.

Little Timmy also presented problems. Lucy began looking to Steve for help with chores around the house. In the past, she had always done the housekeeping alone. He was not ready to meet this new demand. In addition, Lucy was not the fun person she used to be. She was always tired, and the things she did do related more to Timmy's needs than to his. They could not come and go as they had before the baby was born. Invitations to parties had to be turned down. Trips here and there were a nuisance with all the necessary preparations, and often their fun was spoiled because Timmy's needs would prove bothersome. Steve doesn't remember any specific time when it began happening, but at some point he started going out alone. He wasn't doing anything special, just stopping at a local bar after work to have a couple of beers with the guys, or going out to play ball at the park and then having a couple of cold beers. Lucy didn't mind at first, since she did not believe that Steve was getting involved with other women, which he wasn't.

Little by little he began coming home having had a bit too much to drink. Lucy did mind this. When she would say something to him, he would lash back with a fury she had never seen before. The episodes became more frequent. And one day, in his drunken rage, he hit her—hard. She fought back, but because he was much stronger than she, even with the sluggishness of the alcohol, he left many bruises on her.

The die was cast. The process he had so hated in his childhood had started again. Without even realizing it, Steve had become his father. All that he had despised in the past he had now become. Steve didn't see the connection. He didn't even think about it until Lucy, finally seeing no hope for herself and potential danger for little Timmy, separated from him. As a basis for reconciliation, Steve agreed to participate in family therapy. He discovered that without exception, every male in his family over several generations had followed the same pattern as that of his father. All had physically abused their wives, even though they had looked on it with such bitterness in their own fathers. It is almost unbelievable that such a pattern of abusive behavior could continue through several generations within a family system, but it did and it still can.

Steve's story is one among many of those who have repeated a negative behavior pattern which they saw and resented in a parent. Statistics on child abuse verify that most child abusers were themselves abused when they were children. Alcoholism frequently can be traced back two or three generations. Welfare families, those who exist continually on public assistance, tend to carry on the trend from one generation to the next. The child who is born out of wedlock will not infrequently have a child of his or her own also out of wedlock. This list could go on into other problem areas of life to show the giant shadow the parent casts upon the child.

Of course, not all children of alcoholics will become alcoholics. Certainly not all children born out of wedlock conceive offspring in like manner. But when problems within a troubled family are identified, one can see lines of connection to the previous generation. There is a better than even chance that the alcoholic child will be found in the home of the alcoholic parent as opposed to the home of parents who drink little or not at all.

The question raised through the ages in regard to these problem areas has been whether this is inherited or learned behavior. Professionals have taken both sides of this argument, and some have opted to balance between the two. However, no matter which one believes, the influence of the parents on the child is obvious in these situations where parent and child behave alike. If the child learns to go to alcohol as a solution to stress, he has probably learned it from his parent who does likewise. The statement of God to Israel is verified by what we can see—the effect of one generation on the next.

We have been addressing, up to now, some very serious life experiences under the category of sins. These are, of course, extremes. Each of us is aware of shackles from our childhood that chain us into places in life that are simply uncomfortable, although not desperately destructive. Maybe it was a pattern in the home to overeat and all of the family is overweight. They are not really happy with their present eating habits, but accept them as natural for them. They wonder about gland problems; they fantasize about a heaven in which they can eat all they want and never get fat; they read every article about ways to lose weight without having to exercise hard or to diet. But in the end they cut themselves another piece of chocolate cake with gooey icing and tell themselves it's no use resisting because that's how it is with their family.

Spending patterns are another of these potential discomfort areas. Tom had been raised in a lower income family. The family always had food, clothing, and shelter, but never anything more. They always lived from week to week, borrowing for emergencies and struggling to pay back the money borrowed. Somehow they never struggled to save as other people in their situation and income bracket did. Saving was not, in their thinking, an attainable goal; hence it was never taught to Tom as a value.

Rachael was one of two children of a salesman and an office worker. They lived in a better area of the city among other lower middle income families. Rachael's mother was very conscious of what the neighbors thought of her, so she always took care to dress her children well. Their home was nicely furnished, and the parents drove newer automobiles. The children never had a sense of doing without. They got most of the toys they asked for; they got treats to eat with regularity; and when it was time for college, the parents picked up the tab.

Like Tom's family, Rachael's did not see saving as

possible for them, and so never focused in on it as something to teach the children. They felt that people saved to get a new washer, a vacation trip, or a second car, things they had already purchased. They had simply financed them and paid later. "What reason was there to save?" they would ask.

Tom became a successful medical doctor and Rachael taught elementary eduction in the public school system. They had two children of their own, who presented no problem at all financially, but they always seemed to have money problems. In therapy Rachael said, "I can't believe it! With our combined incomes we make a small fortune. Even if I didn't work, we would have a lot of money, but it never seems enough. Money is the biggest thing we fight about. It's crazy. We live in a mansion, we drive high-priced European cars, the children are in private school, yet Tom and I fight over the telephone bill being too high. Someday I'm expecting the electric company to cut off our lights!"

Tom's response was to agree. "Rachael's right. We're not doing bad at all. We live at a level far above what either of us lived at when we were home with our parents. I don't know what it is. We both want the things we buy, but when I see how close we cut it each month, I get a little scared. I think, 'Suppose I became sick and couldn't work for a while. How would we ever pay the bills?' "

This was not a family in crisis. They were not on the verge of a separation or divorce. They were simply fighting over the stress of financial matters. And they were fighting from the preferable position of being well-to-do rather than poor. Many people would feel that they shouldn't have a care in the world. Nevertheless they fought. And although their fights weren't physical, they were still uncomfortable. Each was being faithful to a pattern that had been learned at home. They were living from week to week, not saving a penny for possible crises even though they were in the position to do so. They were simply repeating a sin of their parents without realizing it.

At this point, it must be said that not only sins but also benefits are passed from generation to generation. The other part of God's pronouncement in Exodus 20 is that he would show mercy unto thousands of them that love him and keep his commandments. When a child is raised in a home where a balanced diet is the norm, the person will grow up with an appetite for nutritious foods. In a home where fairness is a family goal, the children will tend to develop their own sense of fairness.

For good, as well as for bad, the recycling process takes place. What we must reckon with is that no one gets injured or has the experience of living out his life "missing the mark" in the areas of wholesomeness that he developed from his parents or grandparents. We need not laud or affirm those qualities within an individual, for they bring their own affirmation and reward. But we must reckon with those qualities that cause problems, sometimes two or three generations down the line.

Within each of us is a part that wants to cry out, "That's not fair! Why should I be penalized for something done by a grandfather or perhaps a great-grandfather that I never even knew?" In order to begin to understand, we need to go back to some foundational principles of nature. In the beginning chapters of Genesis we read of God's plan for reproduction.

> And God said, Let the earth bring forth grass, the herb yielding seed, and the fruit tree yielding fruit after his kind, whose seed is in itself, upon the earth: and it was so. Genesis 1:11

A little later, when Noah is to gather together the beasts for the ark, God instructs,

> Of every clean beast thou shalt take to thee by sevens, the male and his female: and of beasts that are not clean by two, the male and his female. Of fowls also of the air by seven, the male and the

female; to keep seed alive upon the face of all the earth. Genesis 7:2, 3

All life grows from a seed. Whether it be the brutes, plant life, or man himself. Hidden within the seed is the coding for how that life form should grow.

We do not expect fruit trees to grow up where we have planted grass seed on our lawn, nor would we expect the egg of a chicken to hatch as a human baby. We are aware that the natural order is that the type of seed planted determines the form of life that will be produced.

Taking this awareness of the natural order of life into the areas of behavior, we understand that each of us can only give to our children that which we have. And we carry in potential only that which our parents had and so on, back through the generations. In setting forth the principles of his law, God is telling humankind how to live rightly—how to live in such a way that we will not get into bondage and will live in fairness with those around us. Commandments such as "Thou shalt not steal" tell us what is not fair to do to our neighbor and what will end up hurting our lives if we do. Obeying the commandments and statutes of God is simply doing what is right, or righteousness. When great-grandfather decides to incorporate into his life behavior that is not right, he sets a pattern for the emotional seed he will pass on to his children. They are left with the need to carry those weights into their lives and in turn to pass them on to their children. In spite of the fact that we don't like this idea in its negative form (we don't mind that great-grandfather's good decisions affect us in positive ways), we are nonetheless faced with dealing with it in our own lives and the lives of those around us.

We must understand that no one ever makes all the right decisions. We are all plagued with the problem of succeeding in some areas but of failing in others. The end result is that all families end up with problems. Some problems have more serious ramifications than others, and some families have more of a legacy of wrong living than right living, which makes it very difficult for them to deal with their problems.

We pass on to our child the pluses and minuses of our family system. He marries a person who brings with her a loyalty to a different family system. Together they bring to their children the conflict between both systems, doing their best to blend them. Unfortunately, what worked in their respective families of origin may not work in their new nuclear family because there are different components now. What may have been fair in the father's treatment of his wife may not be fair in the son's treatment of his wife.

Anthony's parents were immigrants to America in the early 1900s. They came to this land under the illusion that they would easily be able to work and earn a great deal of money. They settled in a coal mining area because they had relatives there. The major industry was coal, and since Tony's father had no trade, he became a miner, a regular pick-and-shovel worker. The work was hard and dangerous. The pay barely met the expenses of the household. The faith of the family was Roman Catholic and they adhered to the expectation of the church to avoid birth control. Almost every year another child was born until the family numbered twelve in all.

When a family continues to grow but income does not, each year brings more stress on the family. Mother would feel badly that the children would not be able to have, for example, a new shirt for graduation from grade school. She felt caught between the father's demands to be economical and the pleas of the children for that new item of clothing. Periodically, she would buy new fabric and make the article of clothing without discussing the matter with her husband. Monumental battles would arise when he would discover that money he was planning for something else had been spent on what he did not feel was essential. Tony himself had often felt caught in the middle when he had been the recipient of the garment. His father was not an evil person; Tony knew that. He loved his father, but they were living under very oppressive conditions.

Like many young people from the coal regions, Tony left town when he finished school. He moved to the nearest big city and got a job with a utility company. He continued his education and eventually became an engineer for his firm, making an above-average income.

The woman he married, Sandra, had been raised in the city as the daughter of a factory worker. Her family was not wealthy, but they always had enough, and there had never been arguments at home about her mother purchasing special items of clothing for the children. When Sandra and Tony were dating, Sandra thought that Tony was relatively normal with money. He did not hesitate to take her to a movie or out to dinner. He bought her gifts for birthdays, Valentine's Day, and Christmas. She never sensed that there was any difference in their attitudes toward money. As the three children came, and they began to need more and more, she felt him begin to tighten up. At first she would joke about it and call him a tightwad, but later it became much more serious. He would become extremely angry and accuse her of sneaking off to waste money. She had difficulty understanding why he would get so worried about spending when he earned a good income, their house was paid for, and they had money in the bank. In therapy Tony discovered that in subconscious loyalty to his father he had replicated his father's approach to spending, which in his own situation with Sandra was totally unjustified.

Many times as we look into our family system we are caught in a giant log flume that continues to accelerate downhill. The effect of past generations seems a bleak reality, leaving little room for hope. But for all mankind there is hope. For some it is more difficult to discover than for others, but it is there for all of us. We have available to us the resources of redemption, the sources of strength that can stop the downhill race and put us back on the road that leads to a higher way of life.

THREE
REDEMPTION
AND THE FAMILY
Rebuilding a Basis for Trust

The former chapters raised the issue that many people today cannot find a basis for trust in relationship, since they have been unable to find such a basis in their own families. For them their parents' marriage relationship did not demonstrate anything that reflected fairness, nor could they discover justice in the parent-child relationship. As a result, they are afraid to disclose their weaknesses to another for fear they will end up being exploited in such a relationship.

Three questions about justice in a family must be considered. First, because of the nature of family life, there are times when each member will use others in the family to meet personal needs. This means that within a typical family, there will be incidents of injustice and exploitation. Without question one person will be giving more and getting less than another. It is almost impossible that relational justice will always exist. What we must look for is a balancing out over the long run.

Little Jimmy may be given more freedom than his younger sister, Sally, but he may also be expected to carry more responsibility within the family. For Sally to feel a sense of justice, she must see this balance. If she is aware only of Jimmy's freedom, she could feel cheated and become very jealous. In another instance, a young husband and father may exploit his wife and family while he works a job and goes to night school to improve his career potential. He may not give them the time they are entitled to or carry his fair share of the work in the home. However, if he and his wife have decided on this direction, he will be making it up when his work load is cut back and his income is higher. Then he may take the family out often for recreational purposes and may hire someone to come in to help with the housework to give his wife more leisure time.

In this context of eventual reciprocity, we see the family system endure, despite individual situations where fairness does not prevail. A man hiding from the fear and embarrassment of impotence may tolerate an affair on the part of his wife. Because he is afraid to deal with the issue of his sexual dysfunction with his wife, it becomes easier to collude with her in the extramarital relationship. He knows he is denying her his sexual affection, and he knows it isn't fair to do so. She has asked him to pay her more attention, but the more she asks, the further back he pulls. Finally, not because she doesn't love him but rather out of a sense of frustration, feeling that she is not being heard, she flirts in front of him and thus tries to bring pressure against him to draw close. He, on the other hand, turns his head, hoping that this other man will take care of her sexual needs so that he, the husband, won't be confronted with his impotence problem. We can see it is a bad solution, but as the husband and wife live it through, they are struggling for a balance of justice between themselves.

Second, relationships cannot be worked out over a long enough period to get real relational justice unless we move from a "feeling" base to a "covenant" base. Our society has long been locked into the notion of romantic love. We still have fantasies akin to the knight's rescuing the beautiful princess from the fire-breathing dragon and the two riding off into the sunset to live happily ever after. We speak of love at first sight, and focus on the euphoria of a new intimate relationship. We speak of our chemistry "clicking" as though love were something that happens to us rather than something we work out.

These feelings may be good for the dating period, but when people settle down to the nuts and bolts of family life, they need something stronger than feelings to hold their relationship and their family together. They need a covenant, an agreement that acknowledges the responsibilities each spouse has to the other and both have to the children. The covenant signifies that responsibilities determine behavior, not feelings. It is irresponsible to enter into the intimacy of marriage thinking we can cut the other person loose if things do not work out to our satisfaction. It is irresponsible to bring children into the world if we are not committed to nurture and support them as they grow. If we are not committed to the responsibility of faithfulness, then we are sanctioning abandonment—the abandonment of our spouse and of our children and, inevitably, their abandonment of us.

In our culture the notion of covenants and loyalty seem to be fading rapidly. It is precisely for this reason that homes are breaking up and children are being abandoned. If we are to work at balancing justice and finding a basis for trust in the family, we need to move back firmly to the kind of covenant we read about in the Scriptures, which makes our marriage a covenant with God. We become accountable to him to work through it, even when we don't *feel* love for our mate.

Third, we need to realize that none of us is wholly a victim in the life of the family. Justice does not get worked out by looking at our difficulty and the exploitation we have experienced and pointing the finger of blame at someone else. We need to realize that we too have acted unjustly, and that by recognizing our role in the family problem, we can begin to work through our redemption by redeeming those who have been part of the problem for us.

The basis for reconciliation is presented in the Lord's Prayer, when Jesus says, "And forgive us our debts, as we forgive our debtors" (Matt. 6:12). Forgiveness is a process of working out the indebtedness hoping to find a value in the relationship greater than just satisfaction for a wrong done. It is a discovery that there is merit in the relationship and that it will improve if we can balance the indebtedness standing between us and the other person. When the debtor does not have the wherewithal to pay the debt, the only way it can be eradicated is for the other to exercise grace and not exact full payment, that is, to forgive.

Kathy is an example of how this can work. She is twenty-eight years old, the youngest of four children born to a Protestant pastor and his wife. Because of the pressures from the congregation's expectations of their pastor's family, Kathy's parents were strict. As the children grew, they were not permitted the freedom of other children their age for fear they would get into some kind of trouble and bring disgrace not only to the parents but to the whole parish as well. They were constantly watched over by their parents in every phase of their lives. Her mother and father expected high grades in school. Parents told them with whom they should be friends, how to dress, where they should work, how to spend their money, and what they could do with their free time. All of this was not too much of a problem when Kathy was young, but as she became a woman it got harder and harder to deal with. As her brothers and sister married and moved away, her mother and father concentrated more and more on her.

Her life was coming apart. When she came into my office, she was out of work, living at home with her parents, and spending a lot of time sleeping or crying. As we spoke, she began to express real anger at being treated like a child. She felt that her parents treated her no differently at present than when she was in elementary school. Furthermore, when other members of the family would come home with their spouses and children, they too would treat Kathy as a helpless child.

Kathy was intelligent. She had been an honor student in high school and college. In high school she had been involved in leadership positions in student council on several occasions. She had an excellent capacity to reason things through, but she saw herself failing at everything she tried. We began to discuss why her parents had been so strict. We talked about their view of what they had been doing for Kathy. She acknowledged that they were very loving parents. She had always enjoyed their visible affection and lived with a strong sense of security in their love.

We began to talk about her part in the problem. She was complaining about being treated like a child, but she was guilty of behaving like a child. She brought no money into the home, but would ask her parents when she needed money for her car or anything else. She was not contributing by doing any of the household chores. She allowed her mother to do for her in all the domestic areas. Whenever she had a decision to make, she would take it to her parents, who in turn would make the decision.

Kathy began to see how she shared in the responsibility for her situation. She began to see her parents no longer as villains but rather as caring parents playing through the only role in life they knew in relationship to her. Even their vocational choice was a kind of parenting role to people in the church. She began to realize that the other children had taken the initiative to make the emotional break from their parents, but that she had never wanted to leave the security of her parents and so had not made the necessary moves.

As Kathy began to deal with her own responsibility, things began to fall into place. She loved her parents, so forgiving them was not hard. Forgiving herself was the more difficult task, but that too came in time. Today Kathy is employed, married, and the mother of two small children of her own, and has what she describes as a wonderful relationship with her parents. She was able to face the injustice, recognize her part, forgive, and move on to a relationship that is balanced and trustworthy.

Kathy's story was given in a brief account. One should not assume that it was easy to work through or that it went quickly. Kathy was in therapy for over a year and really struggled with the issues of her family life. But Kathy is one success story over against many that never press through that far. Kathy however, had something deeper than her own strength to draw on: Kathy had her faith in God which gave her a basis for redemption and a hope for wholeness.

Whenever we speak of rebuilding a basis for trust in a family, the greatest resource we can link on to is a living faith in God. The issues of looking at the whole instead of a part, of working out a relationship within the context of a covenant, and dealing with guilt and forgiveness are all laid out for us in the redemptive work of God.

It must have been difficult for the Jews to hold on to the feeling of being a chosen people while they were being whipped by Pharaoh's taskmasters and made to make building bricks with no straw. One can imagine the workman picking up a handful of mud that blends with the coating already over much of his body and clothing and mumbling, "Where is the God of Israel now? Did he choose us to be the princes of the slime pits? Why be faithful to a God who isn't even strong enough to keep his people out of slavery? Maybe if I begin to worship the gods of the Egyptians I'd be better off. After all, look what their gods have done for them. They've got clean clothes, and a whip instead of mud in their hands."

We do not fully understand why at times God's people find themselves in what would appear to be very unfavorable conditions. What we do know is that even as our Jewish laborer is grumbling, God is speaking from a burning bush to a prince made into a shepherd, to Moses. God is working out a plan of redemption that transforms a

gathering of slaves into a mighty nation. Scripture records
for us that in spite of how often the Israelites murmured on
their trek toward the land of promise, in spite of their short
memories of the sting of the whip, and expressed a desire
to turn back, God did not forsake them. Why should God
follow through for a people who didn't even seem to
appreciate being brought out of slavery? Why not just send
them back as they said they would prefer? Why even wait
patiently for a generation to allow the young to grow up to
possess the land of promise? Why? Because God made a
covenant with Abraham that his descendants would be a
mightly nation, and covenants are supposed to be kept
whether one feels like it at the time or not.

Centuries have gone by. They killed the prophets.
They turned away from the message of Jesus. Many have
abandoned any form of faith in any God, but God has
held to his covenant. They have been scattered across the
face of the earth. Auschwitz and Buchenwald have come
and gone. But the insanity of a Hitler and the apathy of
much of the rest of the world could not frustrate the
covenant of God. Anyone who remembers the famous Six
Day War is aware that the People again possess the land
of promise and that the seed of Abraham is still a mighty
nation. If, for any reason, they should go under once more
before the end of time, I am sure God will again raise them
up because covenants are made to be kept.

The new covenant carries further the plan of redemption.
It moves beyond the nation of Israel to all of humanity. It
pictures a God who values the relationship with man and
does not want a wall of past indignities to stand between.
He knows that humankind does not know how to get out
of that box, so he sent his Son Jesus to work out the
reconciliation. Our faith as Christians tells us that God did
for us what we were unable to do for ourselves. He paid
our bill in full so that we could start over in our relationship
with him. He initiated. He changed things from our side. In
seeing his hand reach out to us with forgiveness in Jesus

Christ, we begin to find a basis for trust. He gives us a hope, and that hope goes beyond what we have experienced from the hands of other people. It is as well a hope for us to be able to achieve trustworthiness in our human relationships. God gives us a vision of the potential of our relationships one with another if only we can initiate. If we can turn and face the problem and begin to risk giving and forgiving to start over again.

The paradigm of the family is used by God in several places in the Scripture. Marriage is likened to the relationship of God with Israel in the books of the prophets. And it is likened to the relationship of Christ with the Church in the writings of the New Testament. We are introduced to God as a father and are told that all who align with God are his family and are spiritual brothers and sisters. Without exception, whenever this picture is used it is used with the impact of a call to faithfulness within the relationship.

God's desire is for families to remain intact. God does not limit his call to faithfulness to the family, but calls for that same kind of trustworthiness among friends as well. In divine wisdom Solomon wrote, "Thine own friend and thy father's friend, forsake not" (Proverbs 27:10). The standard of God for relationships is that we are permitted to make mistakes and, from time to time, cause offense toward one another. There is a provision for that: it is reconciliation and forgiveness. What God does not seem to want for us is abandonment. In abandonment, a relationship has failed.

One of the unfortunate reactions I have witnessed within the Church has been a turning away from one's family and friends at the point of commitment to a relationship with Jesus. Without anything more than the family's response to the first sharing of this new-found faith (which, quite naturally, sounds strange to them), the new convert assumes that God can do nothing to salvage "that crowd" and so moves on to evangelize the rest of the world.

How precious to me is the picture of God redeeming

Israel out of their bondage in Egypt and into their new life
as his people. As they press on to take the land, they are
told to travel as households. They move in faith as a family.

It is significant to me that numbered among the apostles
were two sets of brothers, James and John, the sons of
Zebedee, and Andrew and Simon. The Bible tells us that
when Andrew accepted Jesus as his Messiah, "He first
findeth his own brother Simon, and saith unto him, We
have found the Messiah . . ." (John 1:41). His heart was
bent on sharing the good thing he had found with those he
loved the most.

To the Phillippian jailor's question, "Sirs, what must I do
to be saved?" Paul and Silas reply, "Believe on the Lord
Jesus Christ and thou shalt be saved, *and thy house.*"
(Acts 16:30, 31). The jailer's response was to believe
them, and Scripture records that he brought them to his
house and there they addressed the whole family with the
message of reconciliation with God in Jesus Christ.

It does not surprise me that he who said in the Garden
of Eden, "It is not good for the man to be alone," and
instituted the system of the human family, would work out
his plan of redemption through families. We should see our
families as being potentially the richest mission field that
God could give us, not simply on the basis of a word or
two of witness, but by living out our new life before them.
We should not write off these loved ones so quickly. Over
a period of years I have watched God touch the lives of one
family member after another until whole families have stood
together in their faith. I believe God has a plan to redeem
families and, in redeeming them, to redeem family life.

When we are experiencing a problem within our family,
we have alternatives. We can focus on the problem and
allow it to overwhelm us. We can attempt to find someone
in the family on whom we can put all the blame
(a scapegoat). Or, we can look at the situation and ask,
"What can I do that will be redemptive?" We cannot erase
what has gone on in the past, we cannot condone what

has been harmful to the family, but we can raise up the hope for rebuilding a basis for trust in the future.

Betty was raised in the inner city. She, like millions of other children, was the product of a broken home. Like many girls in her situation, she married young, at age seventeen, to find something better than she had at home. Rudy was a likable guy. He never beat her, or ran with other women, or drank heavily, as her mother and father had done. They simply saw things differently, and it seemed that every time they talked, they ended up in an argument, and one of them would leave the house threatening to end the marriage. After five years of this, Betty left one day and started a new life for herself that did not include Rudy. Because they had no children, they did not have a need to be in touch on any regular basis, and weeks turned into a year and a half.

When Betty came to me, she had recently become a Christian. She had not really been happy in her time away from Rudy even though she had specifically sought happiness. She had spent a lot of time partying, had drifted mildly into the drug scene (mostly smoking marijuana), and had lived with another man for a short while. She expressed that she was confused because recently Rudy had contacted her and said he wanted them to get back together. She still cared about him, but much had happened in her life. She didn't know if their relationship was strong enough to handle it all.

Betty and I set up an appointment for Rudy and her to come in together. At the meeting we talked about some of the things that had happened in each of their lives. Rudy had remained pretty consistent during their time apart. For him there had been no drugs or other women; in his hurt he still wanted to reconcile rather than dismiss the relationship. We recognized that there was much pain both would have to work through. They could not change what had happened. We talked about the fact that the amount of work for them to do in their relationship made it appear to be easier for both of them to start over with someone new. We spoke too of the cost of throwing away years of their lives together and possibly never finding another relationship that was any better.

I must admit that I was encouraged when they both decided they were ready to do the necessary work. They were scared and uncertain, but they made that commitment. They both saw it as the most redemptive thing they could do in their own lives. We began by a recovenanting session, in which we went through the marriage ceremony again. Even though they had not divorced, they had violated their covenant with each other and they wanted to make vows to one another again. It was only a matter of time before things were moving smoothly.

Rudy, whose faith was stirred through this experience, spoke to me after a worship service at his church where I was the guest speaker. "Last year," he said, "I would have never believed that we could have gotten back together. Today, our marriage is better than it ever was before." They had rebuilt a basis for trust between themselves and had redeemed their family.

FOUR
THE FAMILY AND
THE INDIVIDUAL
Bringing the Pieces Together

Ours is a society of individualism. The heritage of
our country is one of strength and struggle. The Pilgrims
crossing the seas on the Mayflower, the pioneers settling
the West, the industrialist starting out as an unemployed
day laborer and ending up a millionaire—these make up
the image of our land and our individualistic people.

The individualist has matured and become more
sophisticated. She wears designer clothes, smokes a
well-known brand of cigarettes, and drives a classy
new automobile. She is a woman who can challenge
the business world and achieve, operate a household
with children and be efficient, and be as seductive and
feminine as any woman ever was.

In America today, individualism has taken on the flavor
of our contemporary world, but it is really still the same.
"Be yourself," "Do your own thing," "Look out for
number one," are phrases that call us to the role of the
individualist, rather than beckon us to be part of a unity.

It is no surprise, then, that when a family discovers a
member of the household to be experiencing difficulty, the

family will see the problem as being the individual's alone and often urge that person to get professional help. (Thankfully, most of us are getting past the place where we are ashamed to get professional help when we are troubled, upset, or depressed.) The "patient" is then directed to a psychologist or psychiatrist, or, perhaps, if the family is religious, to a member of the clergy. This person is seen as an individual, treated as an individual, and often the family is neither involved nor aware of what is happening.

Certainly, we are all individuals and have our own unique way of seeing and understanding things. We are entitled to be seen for who we are and accepted for ourselves. The problem is that being an individual is only part of what we are. We are also a part of several groups. We are part of a family group, part of a peer group, part of various interest groups (for example, the people with whom we work, share hobbies, attend church).

All through our lives we will face two levels of expectation. One is that expectation which we have for ourselves. The second is the expectation others have for us. Through counseling and by working at change in our lives, we are able to alter, if necessary, our peer groups and our special interest groups. The only group we cannot change is our family. We have been born into a select unit of mother, father, and possibly brothers and sisters. As long as we live, those relationships are part of us even after family members die. We will never have another mother or father. The only brothers and sisters we will have will come out of our family system.

Because a family is a closed system, it is important to understand that a problem is never completely worked out until it is worked through the family. In order to accomplish this working out, we need to understand that there is some validity to how each member of the family sees the situation, even though each view is different. In fact, the full picture can be brought together only when we "see" it from every angle.

Too often, we who work with troubled people get trapped into accepting the problem to be what they present it to be, when in reality they are describing their feelings about what is happening rather than what actually is happening. What they share with us has a basis in reality. If we approach the whole problem only within the limits of their definition, we may get them through the immediate crisis but not help them work through the ongoing pattern in their approach to life.

Leslie had grown up with difficulty in her home life. She was born nine years after her brother and the youngest of three children. She was an adult by the time her parents divorced, but her inner pain was as deep as that of a little girl. Her feelings remained for both parents, and, because she did not live in their home at this point, she was able to maintain relationships with each separately.

She came to me in regard to a question of her faith. She had become an active Christian two years previously and was plagued intermittently with deep doubts. She did not question the reality of God, nor did she question the importance of a relationship with him. The problem was that she could not think of herself as being acceptable to God. She couldn't see a reason for his acceptance of her. It just seemed too easy, too good, to be real. She could believe other people could be God's children, but she couldn't hold onto that feeling for herself.

As we talked, I discovered that these feelings would become most prominent at times when she was confronted with her own human frailty—when she would lose her temper with her husband, when she would "hate" the children for messing up the house, when she would visit the home of someone else and see it as kept more orderly than her own.

We began to talk about her relationship with her father. She loved him, but was always afraid of him. He had a short fuse and was unpredictable at times. He never beat her, but she never felt he approved of her. She always had a feeling that even when she did her best, he was disappointed and wanted more from her. In a very natural way Leslie was transferring her suspicions and her sense of injustice from her father onto God. It is hard for her to think of her heavenly Father without stirring up those old fears within the relationship with her father.

If we were to listen to Leslie's identification of her problem, we would hear her saying she was having a problem trusting God. When we see Leslie not simply as an individual, but as a member of a family system, we see her having a problem trusting her father. If we were to attempt to buttress her faith by going back to the Scriptures and sharing passages that deal with the grace of God and the process of redemption, we might be able to give her a sense of peace and assurance temporarily, but the next time she is confronted by what she interprets as a failure on her part, she will cycle through the problem again.

Leslie needs to rework her relationship with her father and find a basis on which she can trust him, a basis on which she can understand the question of her acceptance from him. Then she will be freed up to trust God and to accept his acceptance of her. She needs to face her father with her sense of inadequacy and her sense of his rejection and hear from him what he felt and why he related to her the way he did.

In the years in which I have worked with the problem of drug abuse among young people, I have seen many cases where a person had to be dealt with initially as an individual. It was necessary for the person to go into a program to be detoxified and to deal with the severe temptation to get high immediately following the drying out period. During this time, the individual needs special personal attention, with a concentration of putting some basic structure into his life to help him stay straight. This approach, however, is crisis intervention and personal support rather than problem solving. Before that drug abuser is able to stay clean on the street, he will have to go back and take a look at his family system. He will have to reexamine the ways he was taught to deal with life and try to rework his responses to a variety of situations. This work can best be done when the counselor can secure the cooperation and participation of the family in the therapeutic process.

Working out such problems is a difficult process. The forces that have produced a particular problem within a family member have been in operation for many years. The members of the family each have their pattern of relating to all the other members. There is tremendous resistance to change even though all say they can't accept the family situation as it is. Some family members have developed the ability to use subtle pressures that at times can draw even the trained therapist into collusion with him. But despite the problems, working with the family as a unit has incomparable benefits. Bringing the pieces of the family together can produce a sense of wholeness in each member, causing such problems as drug abuse to disappear.

Two issues need to be settled in dealing with families as units. First, the therapist must be able to see all sides with a sense of fairness. Second, the family must understand that change in any member of the family requires change in all members.

It is often difficult for a pastor to stand with the family as a whole. His role as an authority figure can cause the children to see him as being like their parents. His position as a churchman can cause him to be identified as judgmental of members of the family that do not practice their faith as consistently as other members. His ongoing friendship with some members of the family may bring him into a situation where he simply cannot be objective enough. Often he can get so involved that he is working harder than the family members to resolve their problem.

The family must understand that all have to change in order to resolve a family member's problem. Too often family members are satisfied to identify the person showing stress as the one with the problem rather than to understand that the problem is much deeper than it seems. When I worked at the state hospital, I learned that "sick people" are only the warning signals that identify sickness within a family system. Somewhere along the line, there were breakdowns within the family structure that possibly contributed to what is diagnosed as a sickness in one of the members.

Ellen was the oldest of five children. At age thirteen she was living in a rural area with her parents and two brothers and two sisters. The family had a few farm animals and several pets on a few acres of ground. Things were crowded. There was much work to be done taking care of home, children, and animals, and expenses to keep everything going were high. Her mother decided to get a job to help with the expenses. Because there were small children at home, she went onto the evening shift, while her husband worked days.

A major shifting took place in the family system. The responsibility of a mother fell upon an inexperienced thirteen-year-old. Her inexperience and the limitations of time made it impossible for her to go to school, cook meals, keep house, and look after the younger children, but she tried her best. The other children resented her being in a leadership role, so they gave her no cooperation and usually made things even more difficult. She didn't have time to develop many friendships, and often felt the need to talk to her father about how hard things were for her. He had his own sad story. He hadn't wanted his wife to go out to work. He felt trapped at home without hardly ever seeing her. Ellen soon found that not only was she being called upon to do the work of a mother in the home, but was being looked to to fulfill the role of wife to her father.

By the time she was sixteen years old, Ellen had been involved in sexual relations with her father for two years.

In exchange for her favors, she was given special privileges of staying up late and going out with an older crowd. The arrangement was disrupted when her father began to give Ellen a hard time about dating a twenty-one-year-old man. The cousin to whom Ellen told her story told her mother, and this woman contacted the police, and her father was arrested.

In most incest situations the mother suspects something, but has distanced herself from her family, and doesn't want to ask questions that might change her life-style. Within the sexual relationship between father and daughter, there is a trade-off. They are both getting something out of the arrangement. These realities do not remove responsibility from the father. He is certainly expected to be wiser than the child and is entrusted to look after her well-being. However, the problem results from a breakdown in the entire system, rather than from a breakdown in just one person. It must be asked, "If the mother had not been away from home every evening, would the incestuous relationship have developed?" "If the daughter had refused to go along with her father, would there ever have been a second approach?" (A fourteen-year-old girl knows when she is being touched sexually, and knows it would be improper for her father to do so.)

The father can be locked away in prison, Ellen can be treated in individual therapy, but those measures do not settle the damage that has been done to the relationships among the family members. If these family members are ever to reclaim wholeness, they need to have the courage to make changes in their own lives. With professional help, they can begin to understand how to restructure their lives and how to rebuild trust with those people whom they love the most. They certainly can opt to separate rather than to work through reconciliation.

In a case such as incest, there are few who would criticize the mother or daughter for never seeing the father again. The reality is that for their own emotional welfare, they should not move in that direction. To leave unsettled a basic life relationship where trust has been betrayed, will only cause problems in every other relationship they attempt to build. They will always carry with them the debris of guilt, shame, and anger unless they strive to rebuild the foundations of trust with the father.

Real wholeness comes by bringing the pieces of a broken family together. The therapist can help the family learn how to relate to one another in more balanced ways, but only the family members themselves can decide to begin the process of healing.

FIVE
SELECTING A MATE
Premarital Counseling

Seated before her typewriter, Michelle was having difficulty concentrating on her work. She never had been really excited about her job, and mind drift was something she always had fought. But today it was even worse.

With her fingers still in position on the keyboard, she lifted her eyes from the page she was copying and looked to where the clock hung on the wall. "Four twenty-seven," she thought. "That means thirty . . ." and after some calculation, "three minutes until quitting time."

She wanted to take another break, but had already had more than her share. All day she had looked for reasons to escape from her desk and let her mind drift into fantasies about how life was going to be when she and Howard were married. She had taken coffee breaks, restroom breaks, candy bar breaks, chipped fingernail breaks. No, she really couldn't leave the typing again.

She forced her eyes back to the page. The words didn't want to get through. With all the determination she could muster, she forced her fingers to begin to press out letters on the keys. "How does anyone ever go on from day to day when they're going to get married?" she thought.

Howard was having his own problems concentrating. He would be graduating from college soon and seeking a career in electrical engineering. These last few weeks of his final semester seemed endless and his course work even more demanding than usual. He had paid for his education thus far with partial scholarships, a part-time job, and occasional help from his parents. Now, with graduation—and marriage—soon to be upon him, he was anxious to get into the working world. However, he hadn't yet found a job.

The night before, on impulse, he had told Michelle that he wanted to marry her in two months. School would be done then, and he felt sure they would be able to work out the details for living together as a married couple. They had met at a rock concert the student activities committee had sponsored three months before. Michelle and three of her girlfriends had come to hear the group. At the last minute, he and his roommate, desiring a break from their studies, had also decided to go.

When the girls moved into the aisle where Howard and his friend were sitting, Howard was quickly taken by Michelle. She told him later that she had purposely come into the aisle first so that she would be sitting next to him. Howard had not been bashful. Before the concert was over, he had set up a date with Michelle for that weekend. Things moved quickly from there. Now they were planning to be married.

Howard pulled on his shirt, slipped on his shoes, and looked at his watch. "Four twenty-seven . . . . Michelle will be finished in thirty-three minutes . . . ." The engineer in him had automatically made the calculation. "I'll have just enough time to get gas in the car and pick her up." At that moment, the thought of his impending marriage once again exploded within him. "I asked her to marry me. In just two more months we'll be husband and wife!"

Driving in the car, he passed a classmate, remembered a test was coming up in that class, waved at the classmate, then turned toward the gas station. It was strange, the feeling he had inside. He knew Michelle was not just another girl to him. She was special. But marriage seemed like such a big move. He wondered if he should have first talked to someone about it, to his parents, his pastor, his roommate, to anyone who might have given him some insight into the matter. Howard had high school friends who were already married and divorced. They had expressed deep, mutual love when deciding to get married. Were he and Michelle going to end up like them? Did they really have what it takes to make a marriage work, or were they planning it because it was socially the thing to do? Were they feeling guilty about their sexual interaction and wanting to give it more substance? Howard knew that "being in love" wasn't sufficient preparation for a good marriage.

He saw Michelle wave. He pulled to the curb, leaned over to open the door, and waited to kiss her when she was seated. Two boys about twelve years old paused to look at Howard and Michelle kissing. "All ri-i-i-ght!" one of them yelled, and nodded in approval to the other. Michelle twisted her head to see who was shouting, but Howard kept his mouth pressed against hers. He liked her feel. He liked her smell. He liked almost everything about her. So why were these questions in his mind?

He thought about discussing his thoughts with Michelle, but he felt embarrassed. He didn't want her to think he hadn't meant what he had said last night. He didn't want to give her the impression that he didn't know what he was doing. "Things will work out," he thought as he sat back from the kiss, put the car into gear, and said to Michelle, "How was your day?"

We would like to believe that Howard and Michelle got married, bought a pretty home in the suburbs, had a few children, and lived happily ever after. That would be a scenario from the pages of a pocketbook romance. However, stories of love and marriage often end unhappily. More times than we care to believe, couples do not live out their lives in wedded bliss. Problems that existed before they were married inevitably come home to roost. Sometimes as late as twenty or twenty-five years after the marriage, these problems arise with renewed strength and cause a tremendous wrench within the home. It is a myth for people contemplating marriage to believe that their problems and questions will go away by ignoring them.

In the counseling room, dealing with couples who are in the midst of serious conflict, often serious enough for them to talk about separating, I ask, "How long ago did you become aware of this problem?"

Often one or both of the people will say, "Well, it was there as long as I can remember, even before we were married."

We are concerned about preventive maintenance on our automobiles. We are interested in preventive education against drug abuse. I would appeal for preventive counselling for marriages which begins even before vows are spoken. It should begin when a young couple feel they have come to the place where their mutual commitment is so strong that they wish to spend their lives together. I would suggest premarital counseling even for couples who don't feel they have problems between them. So often we have heard that love is blind, and yet there are couples who feel that this universal truth only applies to others.

A specific process takes place during courtship. It is pretty much the same for teenagers in love as for older couples who are marrying for the second time. When we find someone attractive, we want that person to be attracted to us, so we show our best side. We smile, speak politely, and do everything we possibly can to make the other person look favorably upon us. The more we get out of the relationship, the more we are willing to put into it and the harder we are willing to work.

Do not be misled into thinking that this "good behavior" stops after three months or six months. Don't assume that it is gone because we feel comfortable with the physical side of the relationship. The walls don't come down until the person inside us feels safe and secure without them. That security usually is not felt until after the wedding, and sometimes not even at that point. I remember words of caution spoken by my parents, and probably by their parents before them: "You don't really know your mate until you've been married for a while."

Marriage is not the only way we get to know someone else well. It is the length of time and the variety of experiences people share together that enables them to get more frequent glimpses of each other's real feelings. Time enables the building of greater security and trust. If, for example, a couple spent a year or two of steady dating before being married, they would generally have a more secure feeling about each other than a couple who marries after a three-month courtship. But even a long courtship doesn't solve problems. It just helps people to become aware that problems exist.

Fred and Kim, a young couple who honestly felt they "had no problems," nevertheless saw the benefits of looking more closely at their relationship before saying, "Till death us do part." They believed that if they were ready to face any hidden difficulties, God would enable them to work them out or would give them the strength to end their engagement. They did not want to spend a lifetime hurting one another.

We started by getting a clear picture of Fred's family system to see what attitudes and expectations he might be bringing into this union. Fred was the oldest of a family of four boys. Both parents had been college educated and worked as professionals, highly respected in their rural community. Fred had experienced very strong feelings of competition as a youngster, but had failed to excel at anything. He was a good student, but was not one of those who got all A's. He could play baseball, football, and the other popular schoolyard games, but he was not the trophy winner.

After graduating from high school, Fred went away
to college. There, for the first time in his life, he became
involved in an overt rebellion against the "right way of life"
his parents had made him live, and began to get slightly
involved with drugs and partying. He started to realize that
he had a lot of anger and resentment toward society, but
didn't know from where these feelings had come. He
became involved in radical politics, which he was always
discussing with a negative flavor, speaking about tearing
down systems and killing people. He knew he wasn't
happy in this, and so he dropped in on a Bible study
group on campus one evening and turned his attention
back to the faith he was taught as a child. At this time, he
as an enlightened adult viewed its teachings and embraced
it because he felt he could find nothing better, rather than
because he was being forced to.

It was in this group that he met Kim, a new Christian.
She came from an oriental background which laid great
emphasis on tradition. Her family, now living in the United
States, was not at all happy about her newfound faith,
but they did not cut her off because of it.

Kim was the third of six children and had always felt
very close to her family. She had never been away from
home for any length of time until she had gone to college.
She was an exceptional student and was, in fact, in college
because she had earned a full four-year scholarship. When
she started to expand her thinking through her college
studies, she felt close enough to her mother to share some
of her thoughts. Her mother told Kim how she felt about
them but also said that she would have to make her own
decisions about these things. It was after much thought that
Kim finally embraced the Christian faith, even though she
knew it would be a problem for her family.

When I met them, Fred and Kim had been going
together for about a year and planned to get married in six
more months. Kim had stayed in school, but Fred had quit
and was working as a skilled laborer in the college area.
He was not happy with his work, but it was the only job

that he was able to get that paid enough to support him.

Fred and Kim seldom saw their families, usually only around the holiday seasons. When asked why, they both felt that their relationship with one another had put a strain on their respective family relationships. Kim and Fred were very active in a local church in their area, and intended to continue with that church after their marriage. Their pastor had referred them to me because he felt that counseling them was something more extensive than he was prepared to do.

After looking at their families of origin for a couple of sessions, we met together for an evaluation. I raised to them areas I felt needed further attention and asked them what they felt most ready to work on. Some of the obvious areas of potential conflict for them were the lack of permission from each family for them to be married; their cultural differences and how these would determine their respective roles in the family; the social issue of interracial marriage; the fact that Kim was an achiever and Fred had an unfulfilled need to achieve; Fred's sense of being trapped vocationally.

They decided to begin with the issue of parental disapproval of the marriage. Both shared that they really didn't know the other's family. They both had experienced immediate resistance from their parents at the first mention of the relationship, and consequently, had chosen a strategy of visiting their respective families alone and steering conversations away from the issue of their impending marriage. When asked why they felt their parents objected, both answered that they didn't know for sure, but suspected their parents were afraid that the marriage might not work out. Pressed a little further, Fred and Kim acknowledged that it was only natural that parents were afraid their children might get hurt in life.

We spoke about the measure of love which such fear indicates, and without question both Kim and Fred felt their parents loved them. Fred, however, referred to the problem of how love was expressed. He thought that he had tried hard as a youngster to be worthy of his parents' love, but had always felt he had failed them and didn't deserve their love.

Clearly, Fred needed to rework his relationship with his parents to discover the difference between his parents' love for him and their approval or disapproval of the things he did. Both Kim and Fred needed to allay their parents' fears concerning the marriage. They needed to make their parents see more clearly that measures were being taken to insure, as well as possible, the success of the relationship. Both Kim's parents and Fred's needed to hear that the young people were willing to take the risk of getting hurt in marriage, just as their parents had taken the risk many years before.

Kim and Fred did not know very much about their parents' backgrounds—their home life while growing up, the course of their romantic relationship with one another, or the reactions of the grandparents to the announcement of their children's plans for marriage. I suggested they find out some of that family history. There might be as yet unknown reasons for the parents' fears that would help Fred and Kim to better understand their parents.

In later sessions, while Fred and Kim were working on communicating with their parents, we took on the issue of Fred's lack of achievement. Did his lack of achievement come from a suspicion that he would fail no matter what he did? Was there a sense of guilt about perhaps becoming more successful than his father? Was he able to see the level of achievement he had reached compared to that of many other people? (He had completed two years of college; his income was adequate; he was able to relate successfully in a male-female relationship.)

Fred acknowledged his tendency to quit rather than to achieve. He wasn't sure where it came from, but needed to investigate further its connection to his relationship with his father. Kim had a strong sense of Fred's potential to achieve. To her, he was a diamond in the rough. Together they spoke of plans for her to work while he went back to school to prepare himself for a career that was more fulfilling than his present job. Not surprisingly, he identified as his chosen field of work an offshoot of his father's vocation. Perhaps he was aware, but I related to him anyway, that his moving successfully into an area of work his father considered worthwhile might balance his father's fears about the marriage.

Neither Fred nor Kim felt any societal pressure about the interracial aspect of their relationship. The people with whom they socialized were basically college couples, and their level of acceptance was high. I raised the need for them to look a bit beyond the present to a time when their children might possibly experience some pressure. This was not to say that their children would be unhappy, but that as future parents, Fred and Kim needed to be prepared to face the reality of prejudice.

Finally, I asked Fred and Kim to look at the cultural implications of their respective backgrounds. For each of us the culture in which we grew up becomes the norm. We don't see the subtleties of our behavior the way an outsider might. To us, the way we live feels as if it was always meant to be. We prefer, for example, our foods; we like our music. Even when a family leaves its native land and blends somewhat into a different culture, it often carries much of its tradition with it. Fred and Kim had to be conscious of the possible conflict in which each would be blinded to the other's point of view because their respective cultural backgrounds were different.

Each area in the life of this soon-to-be-married couple potentially could have gotten in the way of the success of their relationship. They hadn't foreseen the possibilities for harm, but then, how could they have been expected to? Their knowledge in the field of marriage and family dynamics was limited to what they had experienced in their own families. Without knowing where the areas of difficulty might arise, they might have fallen into traps that could lock them into relational stagnation and unhappiness.

Although it is very unlikely, they could find the strength and wisdom to deal with problems as they arise. But why should a couple wait for problems? Why shouldn't they be prepared before the storm comes? They may still get wet, but the chances of marital problems are greatly reduced.

Many churches have a policy of requiring engaged couples to attend premarital training groups. These sessions are very helpful but are often too general to deal with the potentials for trouble within specific family systems. Couples planning marriage would benefit from having their particular relationship evaluated. I am not suggesting that every engaged couple needs a year of therapy, but simply that four or five sessions alone with a counselor can enable them to see beyond the excitement and novelty of their impending union to the strengths and weaknesses they each will bring to their marriage.

SIX
KNOWING YOUR MATE
The Need for Intimacy

Having sex with someone is not necessarily intimacy. It can, in fact, be nothing more than a business transaction between a man and a prostitute. Living together does not require intimacy. Cohabitation can work simply because two people have learned how to live at a higher economic standard by sharing expenses and keeping out of each other's way. Becoming husband and wife can also be something other than an intimate relationship. In today's rapidly moving society, a couple might know little more than each other's name before they are married. Their years together might well prove to be less intimate than their courtship.

Leonard and Andria are almost forty years of age. Married twenty years, they have five children, ranging in age from nineteen to eight. Their marriage is not stormy. They have argued some, but Len and his wife have never physically abused each other. The children are mannerly and appear to function in very normal, age-appropriate ways. The family income level is above average, giving them all of life's essentials and a couple of luxuries as well. From all outward indications there is nothing unusual to indicate that a real problem exists. Yet both Len and Andria knew something was wrong when they came to see me.

Len began talking to a fellow worker who, with his wife, was in therapy. Len was ready to leave Andria that weekend. He had been thinking about it for a while. Their marriage seemed as though there was nothing in it at all. Although he and Andria were living together, in a very real sense, they each seemed to be going in separate directions.

The friend had gone into therapy because six months earlier he and his wife were seriously considering divorce. Though their problem was somewhat different from Len's, they were making great strides in their relationship. It was with this sense of encouragement that Len's friend suggested that Len and his wife go for help.

Twenty years and five children are a lot to walk away from, so Len mustered up the courage to tell his wife how he was feeling and suggest they seek help. Andria was not surprised to hear his feelings. She had similar feelings about their marriage but didn't have the financial wherewithal to move out on her own.

As Len and Andria began talking in the initial session about what was happening to them, they seemed to feel guilty that they were at that place. I asked them how their relationships with the children were, and they both felt that area of their life together was good. I asked how finances were, and they replied that, despite occasional disputes, money wasn't really their problem. I asked about their sexual relationship, and they looked at each other with a smile as Andria said, "We have five children, that should say something." We laughed together and Len continued, "No, sex has always been good for us."

Then I asked the big question, "Do you ever talk to each other in real personal ways? Do you ever tell each other what you're feeling inside? Do you talk about your dreams for the future? Do you share your disappointments? Do you talk of what you need from one another?"

In unison they responded, "No." They described a

relationship in which they had shared some of the most meaningful experiences of life: purchasing a home, giving birth to a family of five children, experiencing the death of Len's father, seeing their oldest son prepare for his own marriage, celebrating birthdays, graduations, Thanksgivings, and Christmases. Together they had experienced all of the stuff of life for the past twenty years, yet in that time they had never really shared with one another their deepest, most private feelings.

When I gathered the children together with them in the next session, it became apparent that the children were following their parents in not communicating feelings. They would talk about events in the home in terms of who did what and how it turned out. They didn't risk telling about how they felt or what these events meant to them.

Needless to say, the absence of true communication was simply a replication of the patterns of Len's and Andria's parents. Andria describes her parents as not being affectionate, although getting along very well. When pressed for what "getting along very well" meant, she responded that they didn't argue much. Her father was out working a lot and mother took care of the home. Len came from a broken home in which his mother had left his father because he was an alcoholic. Len remembers visiting his father after the separation, but he never talked much with Len at all. Both Len's and Andria's families had presented distance as a norm for family relationships. The idea was "don't make waves." Getting along was treating each other with courtesy, but not with intimacy. This lack of intimacy is not at all foreign to the experience of many, many families today. Over and over I hear the words, "I don't even know my husband," or "My wife refuses to tell me how she feels about anything."

Intimacy has to do with what is deep down inside of us. It has to do with stripping aside all of our defenses, stepping away from the games, and, as honestly as possible, entering into a give-and-take relationship with someone else. It means to be willing to admit that something seemingly small and insignificant to others stirred up anger within you. It means to be able to share the sad feelings of a personal hurt which brings you to the verge of tears and beyond. Exposing the real emotional you to another human being—that is intimacy. If you don't trust the other person to be able to hear and understand your feelings, you are not very likely to feel free to talk about your feelings. You feel safer dealing with them by keeping them inside yourself. It seems ironic that lonely people pour out so much of their life's energy on a pet—a dog, a cat, or a horse. One would think that a lonely person should forget about spending time with an animal and seek out a good friend.

When a person has not been able to trust people in a relationship, he turns to a more trustworthy companion. The animal doesn't wound him emotionally. The animal doesn't treat him unfairly. He knows what to expect from the pet and his expectations are met.

It must be understood that the ability to be intimate is either developed or stagnated in the early years of life. We work out our personal approach to intimacy in the home with our parents. Through them we first experience what happens when we share deep feelings. Through them we are first punished or rewarded for self-expression.

Do our parents hear what we have to say, or do they simply reject our feelings as nonsense? When we share a fear, do they help us work through it, or do they laugh at it? If, when we share our innermost feelings with our parents, they treat those feelings with fairness, we are given permission to risk intimacy with others. If, on the other hand, they treat us other than fairly, we feel unentitled to trust any further. We must first work out our trust with them.

Most of us find it easier to hide our real selves by blending into the group than to risk emotional rejection, exploitation, or injustice. We talk about everything except the things that mean the most to us. We move among people as an alien. We become prisoners of the fear that separates our heart from our lips. In our prison we never experience the best life has to offer because we are unwilling to invest our most valuable asset, the real self.

Sometimes the family rewards us for intimacy, and we feel free to share ourselves in the home. In subtle ways, however, the family communicates to us that only they can be trusted at levels of intimacy. We then experience the burdensome obligation to whisper of personal matters so that the neighbors won't hear. As children we feel like a counterspy sneaking out of school while being sure to keep our lips sealed, and then fleeing back to the safety of home when classes are done so that we can again relax with "our own kind."

The pulls within us drive us toward companionship. We want to play with someone. We want to call someone our friend. All the other children have playmates and friends and we want them, too. So we reach out and begin a relationship. Loyalty to family, however, requires that we keep some space in that relationship. We are duty-bound to discover the untrustworthiness in another person, and we do. Our "friend" is put through an endless series of tests until he or she fails. Then we can affirm within us the "truth" that our parents have taught us that an outsider cannot be trusted.

This situation is a sad one in a person's youth, but it becomes sadder and even more troublesome as the person enters his adult years and his feelings of distrust, alienation, and fear flow into these years with him. Even after he has moved from the home of his parents into a dwelling of his own, his inner being is not free to abandon the caution that outsiders are not to be trusted.

Luciele was an only child, born into an Italian-American home. Her parents had settled in an urban area where Italian ancestry was predominant. As Luciele reached her teens, she felt, besides the natural pressure of adolescence, the pressure of divided loyalty to the two cultures which had shaped her life. She was very much a part of the American experience, but she had lived the flavor of Italy in all that her family did.

During the adolescent period, as she attempted to sort through the questions of who she was and who she wanted to become, she was very aware of the pull of her peers toward the mainstream of American society and the opposite pull of her parents to follow in their footsteps. Her parents wanted her to achieve and be successful in life, but they did not want her to leave the Italian way, nor did they want her to abandon the family system.

Luciele's family system was like the kind mentioned earlier—one that demanded extreme loyalty. She was made to feel that her parents were the only ones she should trust. Everyone else was suspect. They were always cordial to neighbors and acquaintances, but Luciele would hear her parents talking behind the backs of those people, expressing suspicions of their trustworthiness. She was aware of the desire within herself to find the right man and to begin family life and child rearing. College life offered her a chance to explore male-female relationships without her parents looking over her shoulder. She attended a school in New England. She did not have to bring the boys home for family inspection and approval, which, when she had done so during high school, had always ended in disapproval.

Stan was her first serious relationship. They met at college. He was from the rural, small town society of the Midwest. He was handsome, enjoyed music and sang very well, was looking toward a career in architectural design, and was the first man who had really made Luciele feel like a woman. They spent much time together since they shared some classes and were always together between and after classes.

After three months of steady companionship, they were both expressing a deep love for one another. As Christmas approached, Stan asked her to marry him. He was planning to give her the engagement ring as a Christmas gift. Luciele describes a feeling of panic at his proposal, one that left her with a slight sense of nausea. She didn't want to hurt Stan and spoil the holidays for him, but she also was not prepared at that point to deal with the question of marriage. Until now, she had imagined the relationship continuing just as it was indefinitely. She could sense the illogic of her feelings, but couldn't deny their reality.

However, she accepted Stan's proposal as well as his ring, but insisted on breaking the news to her parents alone. When she went home for the holidays and told her parents about her plans for marriage, neither one said anything against Stan. How could they? They didn't really know him. Luciele felt, however, a sense of their becoming distant with her and communicating in nonverbal ways that she had betrayed their confidence in her.

Back at college she began to notice things about Stan she had never seen before. Blemishes in his character became apparent. Feelings of being exploited by him began to surface. Even his physical appearance seemed to alter. Before spring vacation Luciele had returned her engagement ring to Stan and they had terminated the relationship with a mutual sense of there being no future for them together.

Luciele describes the craziness she experienced within herself when this relationship of such significance suffered a reversal. A long time passed before she was ready to approach another relationship. There were, however, two more men with whom she became engaged. In both cases she experienced the same pattern she had with Stan. Her parents would become cold. She would begin to see the flaws, and she and her fiancé would break up shortly thereafter.

Finally, eight years after college graduation and four years after her third broken engagement, she met Danny.

Danny seemed to have qualities of maturity and stability that she found very attractive. They lived together for six months. Both were emphatic about not making a commitment, Luciele because she didn't feel she could ever trust someone enough to marry him, and Danny because his marriage had come apart after one year when he was twenty-one years old. For the past ten years he had not let himself forget that pain.

Living together seemed to work out well for them. They had some arguments, but these didn't seem overwhelming. Both Luciele and Danny were in the same profession and shared many of the same friends. Living together enabled them to entertain their friends in a more elaborate style. Both liked the other person and enjoyed being in each other's company.

It was with much questioning that they decided to press their relationship on into marriage. Luciele was determined that she would just disregard her parents' response. She was expecting the feeling of negativism within herself as the time for the wedding drew near. She was determined that she would not allow that old irrational behavior to destroy another relationship. She was determined to make this one work.

Things seemed to go well for three years. They had a child after two years of marriage, and Luciele left her job to spend time at home with the baby. Just days after the baby's first birthday, Luciele's father had a heart attack and died. Danny expected her to be concerned about her mother, so it came as no surprise when Luciele said she was taking the baby and spending the week at her mother's home. What neither of them expected was that Luciele would not return home.

As the week passed, Luciele began to feel that things were not as good between her and Danny as she had thought. She spoke of their not having spent as much time together as before, nor of having entertained as they once did. She now found that most of her enjoyment in life was in the time she spent with her son, Albert, named for her father.

She extended the week at her mother's to two then to a month and then confronted Danny with her desire for a divorce. Danny was a very patient man and told her he would go along with her wishes if she would see a marriage counselor just to sort out what was happening. She knew that whether or not she divorced Danny, she needed help with understanding her life, so she consented to go.

We started by looking at the issue of trust in her life. She identified that the only people she felt able to trust were her mother and her child. We talked about her encounters with trusting people in her youth. She identified an inner feeling of mistrust, a suspicion that if she would let her friends know what she really felt inside, they would not want to be her friend.

Slowly we went back through her romantic relationships. She was able to identify a sense of withholding on her part, a feeling that there was a part she didn't want to share with them even though her boyfriends had loved what they knew of her. She feared their love would fall short of staying with her if she opened up. This same feeling had been present in her relationship with her husband. We probed a little more deeply. She shared how the feeling of mistrust had been like a cloud over her home for as far back as she could remember. We spoke some about the circumstances of her family, how her mother and father had moved to a strange land, leaving all of their family in Europe. In America, they had no one they knew well enough to trust. Given their situation, they could be expected to harbor suspicion. The circumstances of immigration coupled with the fact of loyalty to the families left behind in Italy would call for the mistrust of others in the new land.

Luciele began to see that she was being loyal to her

parents in a situation that didn't require loyalty of this kind. She further began to see that her misplaced loyalty was keeping her from developing her relationships with other people. Danny was invited into the sessions. Luciele shared with him the discoveries she had been making about herself. She expressed her desire to look again at their relationship together. She was not making promises that it could be renewed, only that she was open to exploring how it might come together again.

With Danny and Luciele together in therapy, we examined ways that Luciele could fulfill her need to be loyal to her mother, and to the memory of her deceased father, while at the same time opening herself up to trust Danny more. The breakthrough came when Luciele, Danny, little Albert, and Luciele's mother took a vacation together to a small town in the Southern part of Italy where this family had its roots and where relatives still lived. In her native environment Luciele saw her mother begin to reach out to people with a freedom Luciele had never seen in her before. This new view of her mother freed up Luciele to begin to explore more fully her environment and to develop the kind of intimacy with Danny that is needed to sustain a healthy marriage.

Intimacy is a necessary ingredient for happiness. Man was created a social creature. John Donne's statement that "No man is an island, sufficient unto himself" echoes within the subconscious or conscious mind of all of us. God, in the early passages of Scripture proclaimed, "It is not good for the man to be alone." And so he created Eve that she and Adam might share themselves in a full way, one with another.

It is fair that all of us wrestle with our needs to be loyal to our family of origin, but when that loyalty expresses itself in ways that run contrary to the created order, it ends up becoming destructive to our life. All of us need to learn to develop intimacy. We need to learn how to become free to trust another person in a relationship. One of the profound implications to the notion of God's establishing a covenant with man is that he trusts us. With all the risk involved, he trusts us. And in that act of trust, God establishes the model of his expectations for you and me. He wants us to develop relationships of trust one with another.

SEVEN
SETTING FAMILY STRUCTURE
The Need for Order

Lewis and Edna are parents of three children ranging in age from three to eight years. For some time now Edna has been complaining about the behavior of the children. She feels they are hard to control and finds herself losing her temper with them throughout the day. Her particular concern is that she may hurt them during one of her outbursts. How, she wonders, will she be able to cope with them in their teen years if she cannot cope with them now? At times she just sits down and cries in frustration, and occasionally even wants to run away.

For a while now Lewis has been aware of his wife's feelings. When she starts "coming apart," he takes the kids out for a time to give her a short break. He, however, doesn't see the children to be much of a problem. He feels he has a good relationship with them, and spends regular time giving them attention. He does express that the children's cooperation is difficult to get and that he sees them often not responding to his wife's parenting.

Lewis and Edna are a couple that might very well be considered average. Lewis has a decent job, which provides adequately for his family. Edna does not choose to work outside the home, and with the help of Lewis, other family members, and close friends, she is able to get out of the home and even apart from the children with weekly regularity. Both Lewis and Edna are people of spiritual depth, and are very active in their local church. The problem with the children has raised great concern for them in their attempt to live out their faith. They ask themselves, "Where have we gone wrong? Where have we failed?" Although Lewis is not stressed or frustrated, he is concerned about what he may or may not be doing to contribute to the overall lack of harmony in the family.

As they continue to probe deeper into their family life during counseling sessions, it is becoming apparent that the children are not destructive, nor are they ventilating anger. They simply do not have consistent structure. Edna has admitted that she treats them differently at different times. Sometimes when they fail to put away their toys after being told to do so, she will punish them. At other times, she will simply withdraw in frustration at their disobedience. She and Lewis sometimes disagree about what is acceptable behavior for the children, and the children have learned to play the parents off against one another. Lewis, too, like Edna, expressed that he is inconsistent with the children in disciplining. He tells them they must stop fighting or be sent to their rooms. But when the children begin to cry after being sent upstairs, Lewis will "renegotiate" and tell them that they can continue playing if they behave.

Somewhere in the process of family life there needs to be developed a system of authority and responsibility. If we assume that a person becomes more emotionally and physically capable of dealing with life as he or she grows through the experience of passing years, then it follows that parents are more capable of making sound decisions about what is good for children than the children themselves. As caring parents, we owe it to our children not only to set up the rules that provide the structure of their lives but to enforce those rules to make sure the children benefit from them. This notion is theologically found in all the Scriptures dealing with parent-child relationships. And an added benefit is that it works!

Children need order. Edna's concern that she might strike out at the children in anger grows out of the frustration that they will not follow the rules. However, when the rules of life are not enforced consistently, the children do not know how to behave, so they do what seems most pleasant at the time. When Edna says, "Pick up your toys," the children have to decide whether they really are expected to do so, or whether this time their mother is making noises they really don't have to listen to. In a sense, it is unfair for Edna to give mixed messages and then hold the children accountable. Children have a great deal of difficulty trying to win at the family game if the rules keep changing.

Parenting is a shared responsibility. Both parents are supposed to be passing on to their children the wisdom they have collected for coping with life. It is true that the mother and father have each come from different family systems and do not necessarily see life the same way. The fact is that life is not exactly the same for any of us. However, parents need to teach the children how to function within their family system, the one in which they are all now living, and out of that to learn to develop and deal with other interpersonal relationships. Before the children can develop tolerable behavior, Edna and Lewis must agree upon the basic structure and the particular rules within their home. Such decisions should not take place in the midst of family crisis, but should be established in advance. It takes only a minute to ask one's mate, "Is it all right with you if Sonny plays ball this afternoon?" When the decision is made jointly, Sonny knows that the adults in his family make the rules and do so in a spirit of unity. He need carry no burden for the responsibility of splitting the parents; and he can enjoy his childhood, instead of functioning as an eight-year-old adult.

A major requirement for a healthy family structure is

flexibility: parents need to respond appropriately to the growth of their children. Parenting is a process of preparing our offspring to become reciprocally giving adults, which means assuming an appropriate measure of responsibility. It is necessary, as children are given more responsibility, that they also be given the right to make more and more decisions about their lives until, as adults, they are making all of them.

Parents will often fail into the extremes of giving adult decisions to their three-year-old, or of treating their seventeen-year-old like a baby. Often parents either let go too soon and withdraw the support the child needs, or they hold on so tightly that they smother the development of the child. Being in touch with our children, being aware of them, goes hand in hand with flexibility. We know that a five-year-old child is not capable of handling his own finances. We would not consider setting him up with his own checking account, nor allow him to make purchases as he saw fit. How do we know when he has become capable? We can only know that by keeping in touch with his development. We need to learn to hear our child by his actions, and then we serve him best by letting him handle whatever responsibility he can.

Paul and Cynthia are in their mid-forties. They have four children: the older two are girls, the younger two, boys. They planned their family so that all of the children are two years apart. The oldest, Gloria, is now eighteen. She has graduated from high school and works a full-time job while living at home. Susan, the second child, is sixteen and in her junior year of high school. For the past two years, the family has been experiencing tension over the rules of the household.

What Paul and Cynthia cannot understand is how a closely knit family that has spent much enjoyable time together, could suddenly turn into a boiling inferno. Nearly every week is punctuated by an argument between the mother and one of the girls, or between father and one of the girls. The topics range from dates the girls want to go out on to clothes they want to buy. Until recently the girls seemed to be very satisfied with the policy their parents had set. The parents were nearly always in agreement in their decision, and when they were not, they would spend time working through to an agreement without conflict.

Paul and Cynthia can see that the girls are angry. And they know that when things erupt, everyone in the home feels the tension and gets hurt. What they don't know is how to deal with the situation.

I saw the family after Gloria, the oldest, had started to drink to excess. Twice she had come home mildly intoxicated. The parents were both very angry because they didn't keep alcohol in their home and had never permitted the children to go to parties where it was served. They insisted that Gloria come to counseling sessions even though she didn't feel she had done anything wrong. She felt that there was nothing wrong with drinking and that her parents were overreacting. Nevertheless, she did begin coming into sessions.

As we worked together, we began to discover that the family had begun with some very appropriate guidelines for the children. The children thrived on them, and Paul and Cynthia found parenting a joyful experience in spite of the hard work involved. Cynthia, however, had come from a family in which all but her mother had been exterminated in the German concentration camps in the Second World War. Cynthia's mother, consequently, had a tremendous need to protect her children, a need which became instilled in Cynthia as she was growing up. Paul understood his wife's feelings, and even though he would not have been as restrictive with the children as she was, he felt his wife was entitled to feel secure with regard to them.

As the children became teenagers, their parents did not begin to expand the rules. They had not started the process of allowing their children to become adults. Yet all around them, the children saw their peers moving on into this next phase of life. The children loved their parents, but they strongly sensed the injustice of their parents' treatment of them. They felt the need to provoke situations to draw attention to this injustice. When Gloria ultimately admitted that people drink to excess for a reason, she said that her reason was the despair she felt at the thought of never being able to grow up and still remain close to her parents.

Because Paul and Cynthia were really interested in what was best for their children, they were able to start working out a fairer set of guidelines in the home, a set of guidelines that enabled the children to understand what the parents' concerns were and yet took into account the growth and development of the children.

Most of us do not become aware of any difficulty in our family until a problem arises. As parents, we need to recognize that inadvertently we have created some sense of imbalance in the child's development and that we are now faced with rectifying it. What we have failed to work through with our children for the past four or five years is not going to be worked out at the snap of our fingers. We will not be able to take the totally dependent seventeen-year-old and say, "Starting today, you will be handling everything on your own." Nor will we be able to say to the five-year-old who has been making decisions for the whole family for as long as he can remember, "Starting today, you will do what we, your parents, say." We can say that to the child, but he cannot change that quickly. Neither can we, as parents, change that quickly. We find ourselves falling back into our old patterns of relating to the children, just as we see them falling back into theirs. Change takes time, a good deal of time. We need to view it, not as an act, but as a mutual working through process involving all members of the family.

It is also important in parenting to keep in close contact with one another as parents and, as a team, to keep in close contact with our child.

Nick and Cindy are a young couple just approaching

their thirties. Both are college educated and employed outside the home. Their eight-year-old son, Richard, has been underachieving at school and is generally irresponsible at home. When Cindy tells him to clean his room, he postpones the job until a later time. When she pressures him again, he fusses and moans and resists to the point of being disobedient and disrespectful.

Nick has the same problem with Richard. However, unlike Cindy, when he feels Richard getting defiant, he becomes angry and hits him. Richard, of course, will go do the chore he has been told to do, but because of his anger, does as little as possible.

At school, Richard has been tested by school counselors as well as by a private practitioner, and has been found to have better than average ability. His teachers express that his work is usually correct, but that he doesn't do a lot of it and is often careless. He has assumed the role of class clown, and with regularity is a discipline problem for the teachers.

The simple answer of a tight structure with consistent discipline will not work well in this situation. Richard's behavior problems are not "the Problem." They are the symptoms of the real problem, just as an ulcer is the symptom of anxiety. If Nick and Cindy were to simply lay out the rules to Richard and punish him consistently when he did wrong, they would find themselves growing a paddle as an extension of their hand, and they would discover Richard becoming increasingly rebellious and increasingly dishonest with them.

This is not to deny the value of spanking or of other forms of punishment to make an impression on the child. It is instead to indicate the difference between running regularly to keep your legs in shape, and using running as a means of healing a broken leg. Before you can run on the broken leg, you must have the bone reset and then allow ample time for it to heal. Then the running program becomes effective to return the leg to normal strength.

To simply run on the broken bone is only going to cause extreme pain and do even more damage than has been done. Nick and Cindy were wise to identify within their family system some deeper needs and seek out professional help.

We looked together at the family. We heard not only from Nick and Cindy, but also from Richard. Richard talked about his parents being too busy at times when he felt he needed them. He directed his statement especially toward his mother. He said that when he wanted to get her help, she was on the phone or leaving for work, and would give him short answers or put him off (just as Richard put off doing what he was asked to do).

As a therapist, I found it hard to believe that any parent would be either on the phone or leaving for work at all times, so I pressed the issue further. Cindy acknowledged that she was an active woman, but expressed that her working hours were during Richard's school time, and that the time for her to go to work was also the time for him to go to school. She went on to say that she felt Richard purposely came to her when she was doing something.

We were beginning to get down to causes. As we continued, Nick began to speak about his feeling that Cindy didn't have time for him. As a matter of fact, this was one of the major points of conflict between them. Part of what was happening with Richard was that he was hearing this conflict, was feeling threatened about the unity of the home, and was bringing his own pressure on his mother to stop working and spend more time with his father. When their relationship stabilized, his relationship with them would too. As an eight-year-old boy, he was not able to figure out that these arguments between them were not going to break up their relationship.

As Richard began to understand more fully the relationship between his parents and to know that he could trust them to work through it, he became freer to start working on his own life. At this point, his parents could establish rules and apply discipline to keep him moving in the right direction.

Parental approval is very important. We, as human beings, respond to two major forces. We move away from discomfort and we press toward approval, especially as children in relationship with our parents. The need for parental approval is very strong. Only after much frustrated effort to gain this approval will children give up, as it were, and stop believing in it as a possibility. Parental approval is tied to a child's basic sense of loyalty and with his need to trust, which is most possible in the context of a parent-child relationship.

Parents need to build into their family system the message that some forms of behavior will hurt the child and that other forms will benefit him. It is difficult to expect a two-year-old to understand that playing in the street is dangerous if he does not keep his eye open for traffic. We know, in fact, that he has no sense of concern for traffic at all. So we simply tell him that he isn't allowed to go into the street.

For most parents of a lively two-year-old, this message is not received with an abundance of cooperation. Usually the child will wander into the street anyway, and the parent will retrieve the child and follow up with a scolding or a spanking or both to reinforce the parental message. The spanking proclaims, "If you play in the street, you're going to get hurt, if not by a car, then by me." The child still does not understand the intricacies of reaction time and braking distances for a car at given speeds, but he knows he did something that ended up being uncomfortable for him and that he has received disapproval from his parents.

Hopefully, as time goes by, parents are able to communicate in clearer ways the messages of safety to their children. But the tools for shaping behavior remain the same. Forbidding a fourteen-year-old from going out with friends as a punishment for violating rules serves the same purpose as that of spanking for the two-year-old. It says, "You have done something that is unacceptable, and there is discomfort attached to that."

Disapproval is a reaction that is easy to identify, and it flows from most of us almost spontaneously. Our children early learn the signs of our disapproval, and come to us looking guilty even before we confront them with their "crime." Approval, however, is a message we convey in much more subtle ways. We expect things to be as they should, and when our children do the expected, we often neglect to respond to their behavior at all. They are left with the message that if they want special recognition from us, they will have to violate rules.

It is important that we learn to distinguish between our approval or disapproval of a behavior, action, or attitude and our approval or disapproval of the child as a person. Our emotions, however, sometimes get in the way. We do extensive and prolonged damage to our child if we cause him to feel that we only love him when he does what we want. Labeling a child as "bad" instead of labeling a behavior as bad can be the beginning of a self-fulfilling prophecy for the child. If, on the other hand, we defend negative behavior because we cannot distinguish it from who our child is as a person, we can likewise risk damaging the child.

It is as unnatural for a parent to disapprove of his child as it is for a child to disapprove of his parent. With the same fervor with which a small child excuses the alcoholic behavior of his parent, I have watched parents excuse the drug addictive behavior of their children. If we can distinguish between our love for the person and our disapproval or approval of the behavior, we become free to hold the person accountable for his behavior and to support him through the change.

In the course of family work, I have seen many troubled families with a great variety of problems. Where parents are willing to draw together and work as a team at facing the difficulty in their family and at working through the change, the children usually respond in kind. Parenting also requires the consideration of one's child as a person. The parent clearly must assume a leadership role, and all leadership requires that the leader be willing to move out front as the others follow behind. A parent cannot expect the child to go through change unless the parent initiates that change, first from within. If the parent has the courage to do that, the possibilities for growth within the family system are unlimited.

EIGHT
CHILD ABUSE
Working with the Wrong Tools

Sylvia has four children ranging in age from one to eight. Her third child, Ronald, is her only son. He has just turned five. Sylvia's husband, Ben, knew that his wife had more difficulty handling Ronald than she did the girls, but he shrugged off this observation by rationalizing that boys are harder to handle than girls.

Years ago he became concerned about the physical carelessness he began to sense about Sylvia toward their son. It seemed almost as if she let Ronald get into situations in which he would get hurt, such as allowing him to play too close to the stairway or to use a sharp ✓ instrument as a toy. Ben and Sylvia finally sought help when Ben, on arrival home from work one evening, found Ronald crying because of pain in his arm. He told his father that his mother had knocked him off his chair when he had spilled milk on the kitchen floor.

When Ben confronted Sylvia, she became defensive. She said that Ronald had caused himself to fall by playing while he was eating. Ronald's arm became swollen, and Ben took his son to the hospital for X rays, which showed the boy's arm to be fractured.

When Sylvia saw little Ronald come through the door with his arm in a cast, she ran to her bedroom crying. Ben followed her into the room to find out what was wrong. Between sobs, she struggled to tell him that she in anger had pushed Ronald from the chair. She confessed that she often felt anger toward her son but didn't know why. She hated herself for the way she treated him, but didn't feel able to control her behavior. Sylvia, along with thousands upon thousands of parents throughout our nation, was stuck in a pattern of child abuse.

The cry has gone out from the masses of unaffected persons who ask, "How can they do it? How can parents beat their own child and inflict physical injury? Don't they realize that they're doing something wrong?" Child abuse is a phenomenon that many people don't understand. They see a helpless child who is the victim of an adult who is supposed to know better. Because they do not see the other side, they are confused. Because they receive only partial information, they cannot explain the abusive parental behavior.

The Sylvias of society will never be understood unless we step back and look at the effects of former generations on a current family system. What was happening to Sylvia when she was a child? How did she miss the resources others had to help them cope with their children when they are at their worst? Sylvia carried over unresolved problems from the family in which she grew up to the family she and Ben generated and, as a result, new problems arose.

Few tasks are more exhausting than rearing a child. Rearing several children and needing to deal with problems of different developmental levels at the same time is even more difficult. It is tremendously challenging to cope with the helplessness of the infant, the unlimited mobility of the toddler, the separation issues of the four-year-old, and the socialization issue of those of school age, and the romantic notions of the teenager. This is the complex job to which parents have been called. Because of our social structure, mothers customarily have been the primary parent and have given most of the structure and nurture to the children. Today, couples are becoming more aware of the need for team parenting. The Old Testament picture of families shows fathers playing the active role in the education of their children. A return to team parenting seems to be a return to the created order and hence carries with it some real benefits, one of which is that one parent is not exhausted by trying to do the job alone. Exhaustion can occur very quickly if either parent is trying to do the job alone or has come to the job of parenthood already partially depleted from his or her experiences in childhood as Sylvia was.

As we sat together to consider Sylvia and Ben's problem, the sources of Sylvia's acting out against her child soon became apparent. Sylvia described her home as upper middle class. Her father was an executive in a major automobile industry supplier. He had worked his way up from the bottom, but the climb had cost his family something along the way. Early in his career, when her father was working long hours, taking special training courses in management, and doing as much socializing as possible, he had started to drink habitually. He didn't drink a lot—he was not what most people would call an alcoholic; he just drank enough to "take the edge off." Of course, the edge didn't come off. It was just pushed deeper down. And every now and then her father would explode at home over nothing. Sylvia had often agonized as he shouted at her unfairly for something she hadn't done. He belittled her at times, even in front of her friends.

Her mother, the other part of Sylvia's support system, was not too helpful. Father's position in business required that he have visibility in his community. That was how the game of advancement was played. Her mother became committee chairwoman for several charitable organizations; she volunteered to appear in fund-raising fashion shows; she involved herself in many projects in the local church.

Her activities kept the family name in the media and allowed her father to push on with his career.

There were three girls in the family. Sylvia was the oldest. It became her responsibility to fill in for her mother with the other kids. The obvious question, of course, is "Who filled in for Sylvia?" Many of the things for which she was punished had to do with her failure to manage situations at home. In effect, Sylvia was expected at twelve and fourteen years of age to function as a responsible adult for her siblings and would get scolded and belittled when she acted like a teenager.

Sylvia would fight and argue with her mother. She let her know how much she disliked being put in position of parent, but she was unable to tell her father, who did not take criticism well. Sylvia had watched him snap out at her mother when she said things he didn't like. Sylvia, a small girl, was not about to pit herself against an angry man.

Sylvia's husband, Ben, would periodically complain about things Sylvia did, like buying him clothing he would have preferred to choose himself and taking the kids out to "junk food" places for lunch. From his perspective, these complaints were not serious issues, but for Sylvia they struck at the heart of her role as a homemaker. They undermined her self-confidence and wounded her sense of fairness in much the same way as her father's criticism had done when she was a teenager. Ben had no way of knowing, but whenever he raised his voice, Sylvia heard an explosion of sound that she identified as her father's rejection of her.

Ronald had the sad misfortune of being the only other male in Sylvia's life. He automatically became suspect because all males in Sylvia's life were a threat. It didn't help any that Ronald looked like her side of the family and especially carried some of the facial features and coloring of her father. Sylvia was afraid of her father's masculine power and because of her lack of trust at that level, was also afraid of Ben. It would be disloyal to mistrust her father and to trust Ben. Ronald was another story. He was small. He couldn't strike back. So every time Ronald did something that Sylvia feared would put her in a bad light as a homemaker, she would lash out at him in much the same way her father had lashed out at her. Little by little, however, she began to move from verbal to physical abuse to the point where she broke her son's arm.

This family was fortunate. In many, many cases, child abuse ends in death. Child abuse is believed by some to be responsible for more deaths among children than are automobile accidents or some of the fatal childhood illnesses. In an urban area, with high population density, hospital personnel can testify that it is not unusual for small children to be admitted with parts of their bodies significantly swollen, with serious burns, or unconscious, as a result of child abuse. Most of the victims are under four years of age, and as many as 25 percent of those hospitalized will die at their parents' hands.

Child abuse happens because children grow to adulthood without having been given the proper emotional tools to do the work of child rearing. In many ways, child abusers are themselves survivors of the pain of someone or something abusive in their own childhood.

Sylvia's need was to deal with who her father was. Somehow she had to see not only his abusiveness, but also the merit in his life. She had to go back to her foundational experience with men and rebuild from there.

Sylvia's parents lived in a different area of the country, so they were not available to bring in to the therapy room with Sylvia. However, she was in regular contact through the mail and spoke to them periodically on the phone.

Sylvia began to explore her father's childhood. She started out asking her mother for information, but she didn't know enough. Finally, Sylvia got the courage to ask her father in a letter to write to her about the kinds of feelings he experienced as a child, such as what he thought his parents had expected of him and whether or not he had fulfilled their expectations.

Sylvia had not told her parents about her problem with Ronald. She had been too ashamed. Her father, however, sensed the strangeness of the request in the letter, and along with his response to her questions sent along his own inquiry about her well-being. He wanted her to know he loved her very much and would stand with her through whatever was going wrong. He had confidence that, whatever it was, she would work it out satisfactorily. He closed his letter with an affectionate comment that she was still his girl.

It was no surprise that her father loved her. Sylvia had always felt pretty sure about that. What troubled her was how untrustworthy men were even when they expressed their love to her. It helped her to read her father's expression of confidence because this was the area where she felt the relationship had always come apart. But even more helpful was what her father had to tell her about his growing up. It was almost as if she and her father were plaster figurines cast in the same mold.

When her father was just a youngster, he had experienced from his father the same behavior as Sylvia had from him. His father had been an immigrant farmer who worked hard and for whom even perfection seemed somewhat short of what should have been. The farm was not very big so his father didn't have the most modern equipment with which to work. This meant he had to spend extra time doing things a slower way. His mother got stuck doing all the housework plus some of the farm work as well. She would be especially busy at harvest time when she would "put up" as much food as possible for the family's personal needs. This was also a busy time for Sylvia's father. He, as the oldest child, was called on to help his father in the manner of a hired farmhand. He frequently missed school during these times, because his father felt school was less important than feeding the family, and farming was the only way he knew to do that.

In his letter to Sylvia, he told how he grew to hate farm work and was driven even harder to achieve at school so

that he could get away from the farm. He earned a
scholarship and worked in a factory part-time during his
college years. He knew that his father felt he was making a
bad move in going the college route and felt that he would
never feel his approval unless he became very secure
financially. Her father closed the letter with a very
interesting observation: "In my business, everyone tells me
I've made it; but whenever we go to visit your grandfather,
I feel somehow like a complete failure, like he doesn't
believe I'm well off since we don't own a farm."

Sylvia began to see the pattern. Dad was passing on to
her a sense of insecurity his father had passed on to him.
Because the standards for comparison were changing
through the generations, Sylvia ended up not even knowing
how she could be approved by her father. For her
grandfather, the standard was a farm—that was clear. But
she was not sure what it would be for her in her father's
eyes. It was this frustration, this being locked in a "no win"
situation, that was breaking out of her and attacking her son.

Slowly, ever so slowly, Sylvia began to see that to the
extent her father had trouble accepting himself, he had
trouble accepting her, that to the extent that he was
satisfied with anyone in life, he was satisfied with her.
She discovered from her mother that it was not unusual
at social gatherings for him to speak to their friends with
a sense of pride about "his Sylvia." She began to accept
her father's acceptance of her, and from this point began
to accept her son.

Ronald was seriously injured. We do not know what the
final effects of his traumatic youth will have on his adult
years. By the time his family came for help, he was already
flinching when he discovered his mother suddenly near
him. When her expression turned serious, or when her
voice rose, his brown eyes became large and blinked
frequently. He was already conditioned to her
unpredictability.

Work needed to be done with Ronald and the rest of the

family. He needed to be reassured that he would be as secure as his sisters and that his mother was no longer "out to get him." Five years old seems young, but the understanding of small children can sometimes boggle our imaginations. They seem to have developed the ability to interpret nonverbal cues and to apprehend intuitive feelings.

There is much hope for Ronald, because Sylvia was able to face with courage the reworking of her relationship with her father. She came to the point where she was able to sit with her parents and tell both of them what had happened and how she had felt about them. She also had the courage to rework her relationship with her son.

In one session, with tears running steadily down her cheeks, she apologized to her son. Ronald was not sure, at first, what was going to happen. He kept looking back and forth between his mother, as she cried, and his father, who kept smiling reassurance. Ronald was secure, because his mother didn't hit him when his father was around, but her crying had often been a warning signal for him. When she told him how much she loved him and put out her arms to take him on her lap, he moved slowly at first. When her arms were firmly around him and he could feel her cheek wet with tears, nestling against his, he put his arms around her and allowed a smile to spill across his face.

Children have the capacity to forgive their parents for much. They want to forgive more than parents often want that forgiveness. Sylvia demonstrated to her son how important his forgiveness was to her by having the courage to admit that she had wronged him. Often parents think that they will lose the respect of their children if they humble themselves to ask the child's forgiveness. Nothing could be farther from the truth. A child gains respect and finds trustworthiness in the parent who admits to the reality of failure. It must be remembered that the child who has been wronged already knows that their parent hasn't been fair. When parents refuse to acknowledge their unfairness, they label themselves as untrustworthy to both the child and themselves, and bring stagnation into their relationship. The words of Jesus from the Scriptures, "Whoever exalts himself will be humbled and whoever humbles himself will be exalted" (Matt. 23:12, NIV) work in family systems as well as in the kingdom of God.

This is not to say that a parent needs to spend the rest of his or her life trying to repay a child for an injustice. Once the apology has been made, the relationship of the parent and child needs to fall into place again. Sylvia has not forfeited her right to be a parent to Ronald. She must not fail in the future to set boundaries for his behavior and hold him accountable. She must realize that she is responsible to determine what punishment will be meted out for his misbehavior. She simply must be sure that she doesn't allow herself to slip back into child abuse.

We have dealt here with physical child abuse on the part of Sylvia toward her son, Ronald. We have also raised up the issue of emotional and verbal child abuse on the part of Sylvia's father toward her, and Sylvia's grandfather toward her father. It was pointed out earlier that the victims of physical abuse often end up in the hospital and sometimes even in cemeteries. The victims of emotional abuse often end up as perpetrators of physical abuse and sometimes as inmates of mental institutions, with lives so twisted they never get straightened out.

Do not assume that because we do not beat our children, we do not abuse them. The constant derogatory remarks, the failure to encourage, the name-calling, and the other ventilations of our own frustrations that we spew out on our children, that tell them they are worth little more to us than a doormat, can be totally destructive. The occasional "I love you" cannot wipe away the deep-seated scars.

It is true that many children somehow survive and seem to rise above abuse. But it is also true that many are never able to find themselves and live life out chasing after an acceptance that somehow is always beyond their reach.

NINE
RUNNING AWAY
A Loyalty That Abandons

"Yes, officer. That's right. Five feet, four inches, and about 110 pounds. She's wearing a red plaid flannel shirt over a dark red sweater, and a pair of jeans. No, no, I haven't. She wasn't home when I came in from work, and I haven't heard a thing all evening. No, she's never been out like this before. But, isn't there something more that can be done now? I'm really worried. Okay, officer, I'll be waiting to hear of anything you find out."

Mr. and Mrs. Lewis are parents who take their family seriously. They were never wealthy, but neither were they poor. By both holding a job they were able to provide a comfortable middle income style of living. Mrs. Lewis was at work only when the children were in school because she didn't want them to be at home for any length of time unsupervised by an adult. This arrangement had always worked out well for the children. She arrived home from work, and they came in from school within minutes of each other. She would begin to prepare supper, and the family would be ready to eat when Mr. Lewis arrived.

Barton and Wanda were fourteen and fifteen, respectively. They were both attending a parochial high school because their parents wanted them to be taught about their faith and felt the academic emphasis was stronger there than in their local public school. Bart and Wanda were both honor roll students.

Tragedy had filled the life of this family two years earlier. Rod, two years older than Wanda, had been killed in an accident while riding on the back of a motorcycle. Rod was not identified as "bad" or "wild" himself, but he did have some friends who were thought to be involved with drugs. The boy driving the motorcycle was one of them.

The death was difficult for the family as would be expected. When the grieving process is over it tends to leave a residue. Each member of the family was aware of the change Rod's death had made, and could identify it in the other members. What each failed to see was how these changes affected the family as a system.

Wanda felt emotional demands on her that had not been there before. Her mother tended to smother her with parenting, wanting to know every minute detail of her life. Her father was now looking at her as the oldest child, and consequently expecting her to take on a role of greater maturity. Barton was very heavily involved with sports and used these activities to keep space between himself and his sister. He simply wasn't home that much for her to involve him in helping her cope.

Running away always reminds me of the biblical account of Jonah. God told Jonah to bring a hard message to Nineveh, and Jonah didn't want to play that role. So, he headed out in the other direction. He ran away.

The intervention of the centuries hasn't changed the truth about running away. It didn't work for Jonah, and it doesn't work for us today. No one likes to give the hard messages. We especially don't like to give them to people we love. Wanda felt her family had already endured enough hurt. She saw running away as the kindest move to make under the circumstances. She abandoned them out of a sense of loyalty, out of a sense of not wanting to make them face the unfairness they were directing toward her because of their needs stemming from Rod's death. She was willing instead to let the family see her as the unfair one.

Her parish priest convinced her to return home the next day. The family readily saw the need for professional help. They weren't sure what the problem was, but they knew that something must be out of place to cause Wanda to feel so desperate that she would run away.

As I began to go back with them into the history of their family, several incidents came to light that paralleled Wanda's running away. Mrs. Lewis expressed that she had gotten married young in order to get out of her home. She loved her family, but her father had died when she was young, an older brother had been oppressive to her, and her mother had not been able to handle the situation. Mrs. Lewis found it easier to leave the household than to bring added pressure on her mother by asking her help.

On Mr. Lewis' side, his mother had left his father when they were having problems. There had been no threat of abuse; she simply found it easier to leave than to say the hard things. Mr. Lewis' approach to Mrs. Lewis was to hold his feelings in rather than to argue. He had trouble saying the hard things. Like his parents and sister, Barton had trouble saying the hard things. He knew things weren't good and was uncomfortable with the family situation but didn't have any notion of how to change it.

Running away can take many forms. It can be the flight to a different geographical place, a flight to a chemical euphoria, a flight into the fantasy world of mental illness, or a flight from life itself—suicide, the ultimate flight. We who are left often focus on the pain within ourselves. We ask, "How could he, how could she, do that to me?" Much more slowly do we ask, "How much must he have been hurting to have done that?" or "What was he trying to spare me?"

I do not pretend that all running away can rapidly be

sorted through and tucked neatly into a little pidgeon hole. The point is, we need to consider the implications of loyalty in a runaway situation as well as the hurt it produces. By being able to look at running away from the other person's side, we are able to understand that we are all searching for something better.

I have continually raised up the comparison between the nuclear family and the community of faith, the family of God. The Apostle Paul, in his letter to the church at Ephesus, used a phrase in connection with the growth of the spiritual family. He wrote: ". . .speaking the truth in love, we will in all things grow up. . ." (Eph. 4:15, NIV). The Lewis family needed growth and, in order to achieve it, they had to learn to speak the truth to one another in love.

Healing began when the parents, Wanda, and Barton each shared in the responsibility of Wanda's running away. This is not the same as placing the blame on someone. Each family member had to come to acknowledge that things were not good because of some contribution from each of them. The father had to admit that his expectations for Wanda were often out of proportion, that he kept thinking of her as being where Rod would be in life. The mother had to admit that she was so fearful of losing her daughter that she was reluctant to let Wanda grow. Barton had to admit that he had run away in a socially acceptable way, and Wanda had to admit that her running away hadn't been fair.

Now they could begin to tell each other what they needed from one another. Wanda could tell her mother that she wanted a confidential relationship, but she also wanted breathing space. She didn't want to feel spied on. Mother could tell Wanda that she needed, to a reasonable extent, to monitor Wanda's activities not only because of her own fears but also because it was her responsibility as a parent.

At each point of conflict, a family member needs to be free to say the hard things. He needs to be able to declare that he feels he is not being treated fairly and to ask other family members for support in working out the conflict. The family as a whole must begin to stand together for family survival rather than for each to struggle for his or her own personal survival.

Let us consider for a moment what other alternatives existed for the Lewis family. Let us suppose Wanda had not run away. She would have continued to feel the pressures of the problems but would not have been able to speak about them. The tension within her would have built up and caused her life, in one way or another, to be out of balance. She might have developed a need to depend on her mother because she needed her daughter's dependence. Wanda might have become the perpetual child to the perpetual parent.

Had Wanda stayed away from home, and no connection had been restored, the hurt to the family members would have been like the pain of death. The family would have grieved again, and the parents would perhaps have brought an even greater pressure on Barton, as the only remaining child, than they had on Wanda. The point is, if we do not choose to "speak the truth in love," to say the hard things, we all suffer.

Running away is not just a child's response: it has increasingly become a parent's reponse to children, or a husband or wife's response to a mate. In family after family one of the parents has disappeared—just packed up and left. We all need to see clearly that we don't run away from someone else; we run away from ourselves. When we are not happy or satisfied with the way we behave toward the people around us, we run from that image we have of ourselves.

The psalmist says to God, "Where can I flee from your presence?" (Ps. 139:7, NASB). The problems that you run away from, the problems that are you, are an awesome presence. No matter how far you go, you cannot hide from yourself. You can flee a thousand times, but still you have not escaped. Because you cannot escape. Your only hope is to go through the hard work of change.

We need also to understand that love does not imprison its object. Fear imprisons its object, insecurity imprisons its object, anger imprisons its object, but love does not. It is foolish for a parent to think that he can prevent a child from running away by placing greater restrictions on the child. Many times a child who has run away once will do so several times again in spite of the problems with police, the beatings at home, and the threats of worse.

Husbands or wives cannot prevent a mate from running away by threats of abuse, infidelity, or reciprocal abandonment. The family system can only work when there is an ongoing attempt to be honest and fair. Parenting is hard, very hard. Marriage is hard. It demands sacrifices all along the way. But the reality is that life is hard. There is a price to pay for every decision we make. To live in a family system that chooses fairness over other choices is to live a happier life than the other ways can provide.

We do not run away from happiness. We do not run away from people whose attitude toward us is fair, who practice reciprocal sharing and allow us the freedom to choose. We run away from unfairness, from those who will not allow us to be free.

Freedom, however, does not mean anarchy. A home needs structure. It should not be assumed that a family unit can be open-ended with members coming and going without accountability to one another. Certain demands must be worked out. There must be a balance. With a child the balance is not simply imposing on him the expectations of the parent. We cannot expect our son to be interested in classical music because we liked it when we were his age. We cannot expect our daughter to want to care for the family pet because her mother did so at her age. We need to discover the capacities and potentials of our children and hold those out to them to achieve.

Mr. and Mrs. Lewis were having difficulty seeing Wanda

as the person she really was. Their temptation was to see her as sketched by their needs and by their lack of faith in her ability to work through her own life. Wanda felt trapped, and so she ran. Fortunately, her respect, born of love for her parents, allowed the priest to convince her to try to talk through her difficulties with her parents. Also, she felt a greater desire to be with her family than to face the loneliness of staying away.

However, she could have made it alone. Many young girls have stayed away until they were legally old enough to prevent their parents' bringing them back. We should not make the mistake of thinking that our child would not be willing to make the sacrifices necessary to stay away. Unfortunately, children often feel they are making these sacrifices for the sake of their parents. They feel that everyone is better off without them in the household.

When a child, a husband, or a wife begins to talk about leaving, we need to listen and find out what is really beneath those words. We should talk openly about how we would honestly feel if the person left. We should talk about what we want from him if he should stay and what we are willing to give in return. We shouldn't just talk. Nor should we get into the crisis intervention syndrome of saying what the person wants to hear in order to calm him down. This approach does not change anything in the long run. We should sort out our thoughts and "speak the truth in love," and be willing to stand by what we agree to do.

Somewhere a line must be drawn. There is a place beyond which we should honestly feel we cannot go. We have done our best to understand the other person's feelings. We have been relatively consistent in upholding our side and honestly feel we have been fair. We feel, on the other hand, that our child or spouse or whoever is threatening to run away hasn't been fair or consistent. We need to be willing to say, "If we cannot work through this problem, and you feel the need to go, you are free to do so."

This is not a position of weakness. It is a recognition of reality. As we expressed earlier, there is no way to make a person stay with us. And, when we consider everything, the final reality is that we cannot make a person stay alive. If we block his or her path from one form of running away, there's always the unalterable route—suicide.

TEN
HOMOSEXUALITY
The Implications within a Family

Today, Lorraine told Vincent, her husband, that she is gay. They have two small children. Their marriage is over. Vince will spend the next several years trying to reestablish the relationship and in the process, to deal with the impact of this revelation on his self-image. Afterwards, he will attempt to move on in life.

Homosexuality is one of the most difficult issues the human community has had to face. There is no positive proof concerning its origins. It looms as a threat to the sexuality of heterosexuals, and has a way of arousing hostility from both points of view as few other issues of life-style can.

My intention is not to make all-encompassing statements about human sexuality. It is foolish to assume that an issue as complex as sexual identity can be dealt with exhaustively in one chapter of a book and from one point of view. My intention is to raise several questions about homosexuality from the perspective of family life and to attempt to lend some deeper understanding to what may take place inside a person who has chosen to live out a homosexual life-style.

To clear the air, let us deal first with homosexuality and the Christian faith. Two issues must be raised, the question of homosexuality as sin and the manner in which the church chooses to deal with those who do not meet the standard.

To understand sin we must return to the Scriptures and look at the transition in life for mankind when sin entered the Garden of Eden. Before Adam and Eve's disobedience, life in Eden was peaceful. Man lived in harmony with nature. He did not raise up his hand against the animals, nor did the earth "bring forth thorns and thistles." Eden was, as described, a paradise where man communed with God.

At the point where man chose to go contrary to the instructions of God for his life, all of creation lost its harmony. The curse of sin worked its way through human society, the animal kingdom, and into the earth itself. Plagues, droughts, disease, birth defects, have all been the effects of the curse of sin on the created order.

If we accept the concept of sin as "missing the mark," then we will see that whatever is not in harmony with God's created order will carry with it grave consequences. Man's sin is seen in the pollution of our air and water, in the wars that have taken the lives of millions, in global hunger and poverty.

Part of Christian belief is the willingness to accept God's revelation by faith. If, before we can accept Scripture, we feel the need to understand it thoroughly, we are setting ourselves up as the standard for truth and demanding that God's Word fit into our standard. We need not necessarily understand why God gives specific instructions, but we need to accept that there are reasons why he does. The law of circumcision, many years after the giving of the command, was discovered to have medical benefits. The dietary laws prohibiting the eating of pork prevented disease about which those who obeyed the law never knew.

The strongest argument against homosexuality as a way of life is that it is contrary to the natural order of creation. Scripture gives us a picture of God creating male and female for each other. To choose a way contrary to this must carry costs. From the perspective of "missing the mark," it is sin. However, so is much of the behavior seen regularly within the church congregations. Greed is sin. Gossip is sin. Gluttony is sin. Heterosexual lust is sin. Bitterness is sin. The list could go on and on.

Many Christians attempt to separate the homosexual from other sinners on the basis of strong biblical prohibitions against "unnatural affection." However, even though it is dealt with as unnatural and sinful, homosexuality is frequently mentioned in passages that identify other areas of man's missing the mark. We need to remember that homosexuals are people. We need not condone their life-style to appreciate their value as human beings, as creations of God, made in his likeness. Also, we need to remember that the redemptive work of Jesus was carried out for all of mankind, not for just a selected group of sinners. The healing power of God is there for us whenever and however we miss the mark.

Mine is not an argument for gay rights, but for human recognition. I am not asking us as Christians to endorse homosexuality, but to try to understand this problem in the same way that we try to understand the glutton, the gossip, and the person with inner anger. I do not argue on behalf of sin as the intended condition of man, but rather as the condition in which all of us partake.

I have felt some of the pain radiating from people who have come to me with the problem of homosexuality. Esther speaks of herself as having been homosexual as long as she can remember. Her earliest recollections of sexual experience are of what occurred between her and her sister. Her sexual interest continued strongly from these experiences. They were always pleasant as she recalls, and were always at the edge of her mind.

At age twenty-seven, Esther describes herself as getting along well with males but of their having absolutely no sexual attractiveness for her. She does, on the other hand, find women very stimulating sexually. She says she is a confirmed lesbian.

What was interesting to me, as she spelled out her story, was that there were several significant messages that she had received from her family as she grew up that carried loaded sexual implications. The fact that she and her sister had engaged in mutual masturbation periodically was relatively minor. Many children have their earliest sexual experiences with some one of the same sex, often a sibling, and never have a sense of being homosexual. Esther had read more into that act than was necessary.

When she was a very small child, her father left home. Her mother remarried shortly thereafter. Esther refused to take on the surname of her stepfather, as her older brother and sister had, but clung to the name of her father. A great deal of conflict arose between Esther and her mother over the issue of her loyalty to her father.

As a young teenager, Esther managed to track down her father and speak to him. He was cold and distant, and told her that he didn't believe she was really his child. He accused her mother of promiscuity and of getting pregnant by another man. Esther looked very much like her mother, and resembled the man she thought was her father very little. But she refused to accept that he was not her father.

Adopted children frequently desire to fasten themselves to a set of natural parents. These children are questioning their basic worthiness. "What was wrong with me that my parents gave me away?" they ask.

This inner struggle took place in Esther throughout her teens. Although she was the family outcast, the black sheep, it was very important for her to be identified with the same natural parents as her older brother and sister.

An interesting phenomenon takes place within people after they marry but before they begin to have children. When someone asks them how their family is doing, they associate "family" with their mother, father, and siblings. After the first child is born, they begin to associate "family" with the new unit of themselves, their spouse, and their child.

Because a homosexual relationship precludes a child's being born from that union, it becomes a "safe" relationship for the person who needs to hold on to his or her identification with the family of origin. This does not imply that all people with this loyalty need will choose to become homosexual, or that all homosexuals are dealing with this loyalty issue. It is simply to say that Esther had to fight for a very basic identification which most of us simply assume. Homosexuality for her is the manifestation of an issue of loyalty. Unless she can work through to a feeling of being secure in her family relationships, she may never be free to enter into a "normal" life-style.

Pete's experience shows us another side of loyalty. From childhood through adulthood, he displayed heterosexual behavior. From his youth, he had always felt closer to his mother. He saw his father as the unfair one because he was often out of the house in the evenings, and his mother was always especially tense when he didn't get home on time. Frequently, the parents would argue when his father got home.

When Pete reached his later teens, the situation at home seemed to settle down. His father became ill and eventually stayed home not only in the evening, but also during the day. Because of the seriousness of his illness, he had to stop work and remain at home.

Pete watched his father's deterioriation from a distance. In the eleven years from the diagnosis that his father had cancer to his father's death, Pete went away to college, met and married his wife, had two sons, and became established in a career as a social worker. As his father became progressively weaker, there were times when Pete felt his father wanted to spend more time with him, but Pete didn't want the closeness. He was still somewhat angry at his father for the problems of the past, during which time his father had put space between them.

In a deathbed confession, his father "came out of the closet." In their last conversation alone, he disclosed that he was homosexual. He and Pete's mother had had only a brief period of sexual activity in their early married life and that he had become "unable to perform." He then told of how feelings he had had as a youngster made him realize that he was more stimulated by men than by women. He told Pete that he and his wife had agreed to stay together for Pete and to keep this information from him. Dad expressed that gay life had been very problem-laden for him. He was glad that Pete had not been affected in this manner, and he asked Pete's forgiveness for failing to have a better relationship with him. He had been afraid of influencing Pete toward homosexuality or of causing him to feel he was an outcast because his father was gay.

Pete was twenty-six at the time of his father's death. By the time he was thirty, he was divorced from his wife and readily identified himself as a homosexual.

When I spoke with him, Pete was in his middle forties, had been in and out of a multitude of relationships with gay lovers, and was feeling an emptiness from the life he was leading. We began to speak about how he had concluded that he was gay. He, like Esther, alluded to an early encounter with a neighbor boy with whom he had been friends all his life. During play, the boys went into the basement of the neighbor's home and there he, at the suggestion of the other boy, had submitted to mild sexual playing. Pete remembered how pleasant it had been to him, but had been ashamed even to allow himself to acknowledge these feelings. He never talked to anyone about the experience, not even to his wife.

When his father was sharing the secret of his own homosexuality, this memory flashed through Pete's mind. He immediately put the thought out of his mind, but it rested as an ache somewhere in the darkness of his subconscious. Although he told his father that he forgave him for not spending more time with him when he was young, Pete really felt contempt, shame, and bitterness.

Pete described his father's funeral as a time when he kept himself emotionally separated from the event. He said that when he would start to think, he felt as if he would go out of his mind. He told of a chaos of emotional feelings, like clay of different colors inseparably mixed together. He did not cry. He did not grieve. He simply kept himself detached.

In the months that followed, he began to have recurring dreams of being approached by a homosexual. He would wake up repulsed, but also sexually stimulated. He started having difficulty in lovemaking with his wife. In the middle of intercourse, he would begin to get periphal flashes of his homosexual dream and would be unable to sustain an erection.

He did not discuss these thoughts and feelings with his wife. He was afraid of scaring her with the possibility of his being homosexual and he was ashamed of what his father had been. Instead, Pete gradually stopped approaching his wife for sex. She sensed that something was wrong and tried one or twice to bring up the subject of their sex life. But he quickly cut off discussion by saying that he was dealing with a very heavy case load at work and just couldn't concentrate at that point. He assured her that everything would be all right.

The dreams continued, and Pete began to give in to the proposition from the unknown solicitor. He began to experience stimulation and pleasure in the dream, but still fought these thoughts in his conscious hours. Finally, his wife, after a year of no sexual activity, gave him an ultimatum. Either he would go with her to a marriage counselor or she would separate from him. He was still not able to face his problem openly, and so she left.

It was during this time alone that he met a young man in a bar. They began to share time together out of mutual loneliness, and in a short time each identified strong feelings for the other. They began living together. Pete came out of the closet. His wife, of course, divorced him and tried to find a new life for herself. She never remarried, although she had several male companions.

The argument may be made that Pete had latent homosexual tendencies that were genetically passed to him through his father. Pete said he had discovered that his father's father was also involved in homosexual behavior. But there are other influences that must be considered, namely, the implications of family loyalty that arise in Pete's situation.

Typically, when a parent-child relationship has not been worked through at the time the parent dies, the child is left with a sense of guilt. How does a child then repay the debt to the deceased parent? In Pete's situation, his father's confession, although offensive to Pete, enabled him to see his father's intention to shelter him. Pete then felt guilty because he held anger toward his father for many years on a false premise. His anger was not based on fact, but on what he surmised was a desire on the part of his father to be unencumbered by the need to spend time with his son. By imitating his father's homosexual behavior and by putting space between his own wife and children, he implied that his father was not all that bad because he, Pete, was like him.

Pete is in pain. He doesn't want to be gay, but at this point he doesn't know how to change. There is, however, hope for Pete. But the way is a difficult one. Pete needs to go back in time. He needs to forgive his father. He needs to recognize that, given his father's situation, his father did the best he could. The way life worked out for Pete was not ideal. But he needs to recognize the merit of his father's motives. If Pete can be loyal to his father at the level of understanding, he no longer needs to demonstrate a loyalty by imitation.

We have thus far discussed two loyalty implications that can play a part in someone's move into homosexuality: The need to hold on to identity with one's family of origin, and the need to repay an indebtedness to a homosexual parent. There is yet another area of family life that can have an effect.

Ralph was the second of three sons born to a lower-income family. The male model in his community was the macho man. His father had been a corner boy and had a reputation in the neighborhood for having been tough. Ralph's older brother liked sports and did quite well. The father would encourage this son by playing outdoors with him as well as by bragging to other people about his son's achievements. Ralph's younger brother was a corner boy as his father had been. He got into trouble at school. He fought often on the streets, and, even though he was always making problems for his parents, this brother, Ralph could sense, had his father's approval.

Ralph was the "different one." He was sensitive as a child and would cry when he was either physically or emotionally hurt. He liked beautiful things, such as clothes and paintings. He enjoyed music and spent a lot of time alone learning about music theory. He learned to play competently several instruments, although he was not an accomplished musician. All of these interests were foreign to his father, and so he rejected them.

From as far back as he can remember, Ralph recalls his father calling him a sissy. His brothers later picked up the theme and changed the label to "faggot." He was driven continually to his mother for comfort and love. Because he and his brothers were close in age, the label of "faggot" moved through his peer community, both at school and in the neighborhood.

When Ralph was fourteen, his father died from a heart attack. Ralph recalls a feeling of hopelessness. He never had felt loved by his father, and yet he so badly had wanted that love. At seventeen, Ralph had his first sexual encounter. He got together with a girl from the neighborhood. She was on uppers and invited him to bed. He was unable to get an erection and decided that what he had been told about himself for years was actually true. He was a homosexual.

He went through several years as a closet gay, limiting his sexual activities to short, clandestine affairs. Out of his unhappiness, he sought help and came to me to work through his problem. We went back to his relationship with his father, or, more appropriately, to his lack of relationship with his father. We spoke about his father's limited notion of masculinity and how hard it had been for his father to understand a fuller concept of manhood. We spoke about the difference between feeling love for a man and expressing sexuality with a man. Slowly Ralph identified that he had yearned as a child to hug his father and to be hugged and held in return. He spoke about how, in his homosexual involvements, he liked the affection part, but felt uncomfortable and guilty, and sometimes even experienced a death wish when performing sexual acts. He was homosexual because he needed love from a man, his father. His "lovers" were the closest he could come to that love.

Ralph was able to move on to an acceptance of himself as a man. He came to understand that his father had loved him, as well as his brothers, but his father had been uncomfortable, perhaps threatened, by the things that had interested Ralph, and had pushed hard to involve Ralph in more familiar activities. The space was there between father and son because the father hadn't known how to cross it.

For a year and a half, Ralph was in therapy working through this issue. He now identifies himself as a heterosexual. He is comfortable dating women. He finds femininity sexually stimulating and is looking forward to marriage and fatherhood at some point in the future.

Ralph may yet have problems to face. He is still aware of the side of him that can be sexually stimulated by a male companion. He may be faced at some point with the need to speak to a perspective mate about his previous sexual orientation. He may meet and have to deal with solicitation from "lovers" of the past. Ralph is aware of these potential problems, but he is committed to press ahead. He credits his relationship with God for the wholeness he now feels in his life, and believes that God will not let him down as he continues to work at his life.

ELEVEN
THE MYTH OF THE AFFAIR
A Symptom of Relational Infidelity

Susan could tell that something was wrong. Every time she and Art were alone she sensed a distance. He had difficulty maintaining eye contact with her, and there was a sadness in his eyes that had not been there before. At first she didn't think much about the time he was spending away from home. His job had always kept him on an erratic schedule, and periodic travel was a condition. He never spoke much about his job or, for that matter, even the people with whom he worked.

But she had noticed a change. It wasn't a thunderclap. It was more like the quietness that comes in the night when an intruder is moving through the woods. If someone had asked her to be specific, she would not have been able to identify anything in particular. There was no lipstick on the collar, no smell of a strange fragrance, no reports from anonymous callers. Nothing. Nothing, that is, but that feeling—the feeling that comes after living with someone for fifteen years, and just knowing that something is different.

Art was having an affair. It had started as a casual thing. Every morning for years he had stopped at a diner near his office for coffee and a Danish. He would use this time to go through his newspaper and get himself in the proper frame of mind for work. About a year before, a new girl had begun working behind the counter. She was several years younger than Art, was divorced, with no children, and had found Art very attractive.

The initiative was on her part. She had come back, after serving some other customers, to begin a conversation, while wiping down the counter as a pretext for being in that area. Her attention flattered Art. He never imagined that someone so young and pretty would be interested in speaking with him, let alone find him attractive.

Through the day he found it difficult to fasten his attention on his work. The idea of her was like a kitten playing with the shoelace of his mind, pulling out the bow each time he retied it. On the periphery of his thoughts he had remembered the pleasure of her company. He sat at the counter the next morning, and again they played. Breakfast became dinner and dinner, bed.

As the year went by, the expectations of the "other woman" grew. She wanted to see him more. She wanted to be close to him in ways that a wife is close to her husband. She wanted to share greater confidences than just the confidence of their relationship. She wanted to gain that first place within his heart that he had reserved for his wife, Susan.

It came to him suddenly one day. He realized that he was being more honest to his lover than he was to his wife. There was a hurt inside, because he had never intended for the relationship to become that intimate. He had not started out with even a conscious desire to be dishonest with Susan. It was hard for him to figure out where it had come from, because he had always felt he and Susan had a good marriage. They both loved the children and had together planned to have them. They lived at a better than

average economic level, and they seldom fought, and then
only about little things that seemed insignificant in their
marriage. It was this inner conflict that cried for a way
out for Art, that Susan had begun to feel.

Susan was afraid to raise the question, first because of
the issue of the shame, and secondly because of the fact
that she had no hard evidence. It was Art who broke
through one evening after the children were in bed. He
couldn't keep his mind on the TV any longer, and the pain
of carrying his guilt in the presence of Susan became too
great. He began to weep as he told Susan he was going
to leave. He told her he felt rotten, that his life had never
been so miserable. He spoke briefly about there being
another woman, but that he wasn't sure if he loved her
or not. He was just confused and had to have some time
to clear out his thoughts—to somehow stop hurting all
the people he cared most about.

Art and Susan's problem is not uncommon. Sexual
infidelity is an experience that thousands and thousands
of marriages face each year. There are no standard types
to whom we might expect to limit it. It happens among
the poor and the wealthy, among the nationally-known
Hollywood personalities and the neighbors on our street.
It happens to newly married couples and to couples who
have been married a long time. It happens to the
nonreligious and within the religious community as well.

Something should be said about mid-life crisis. Art was
thirty-eight and his lady friend twenty-six when their affair
began. Art was facing the struggle of the man against the
aging process, a battle he can never win but one which
often scares him into a valiant fight. It can be argued that
Art was living through a time of reevaluation, but there
was an even deeper cause for his problems.

Art had grown up in a troubled home. His parents
had fought a lot. Art had been his mother's advocate over
against his father. When Art was fifteen, his mother and
father separated and were finally divorced. Art lived with

his mother and remembers the pain and anger within her over the divorce. She would never outrightly say it, but she often implied that her husband had run around with other women. She was very active in her faith and always told Art he should honor his father, but he could never seem to understand what she meant since she herself never spoke well of her husband. She would either imply something negative, or simply say nothing.

From time to time, Art would see his father. He wanted very much to find the courage to confront him about the unfaithfulness issue, but he never did, and so never could let go and forgive him. Through the years, Art had little to do with his father and hardly spoke of him to other people. When he did, he, like his mother, implied that his father was an evil man.

At still another level there was something else at work in Art's behavior. Because Art's mother was religious, she directed him very strongly toward his own involvement in the church. He had gone to a strict, church-related school, and had carried his virginity into marriage. This was not the case with Susan. Her parents had been very permissive with her through the teenage years, and, although they would never have openly permitted her to have sex, she had the freedom that allowed a sexual liaison to happen. She had had several sexual experiences before she married Art. She had told Art of these relationships before they were married, even though she feared they might make a difference to Art. But he expressed the attitude that the past was the past and that it didn't bother him.

However, within himself he recognized the unquiet feeling that Susan had participated in something his loyalty to his mother had kept him from. He had a deep inner sense of resentment that Susan had had those experiences, and jealousy that he had not. After the time they had spoken about her sexual experiences, neither Art nor Susan had ever mentioned them again. There was, in fact, a felt sense of steering away from the subject, a silent agreement to say nothing more about it.

Art's affair, however, broke their unspoken pact. It raised the question of their faithfulness to each other in different areas of their lives. Why had they never trusted each other enough to talk about the problems of sex in the past? What were they missing together that left space for an outsider to enter into their relationship?

The affair also did something in Art's relationship with his parents. It was, to his recollection, the first time he had done something serious enough to earn his mother's disapproval. He was thus separating from her emotionally in a way that most teenagers separate emotionally from both parents. It was also an act, which, in spite of the huge costs to many people, connected him inwardly to his father. For the first time in his life, he began to feel some sense of understanding that perhaps his parents' troubled marriage wasn't all his father's fault, that maybe his father shouldn't simply be explained away as evil by him and his mother.

So that we do not get bogged down in the issue of the good or evil of sexual infidelity, we must understand that God calls us to fidelity, and infidelity at any level of any of our relationships is always corrupting, or, perhaps more accurately, indicative of a corruption that already exists. This is not an issue of right against wrong, but rather of an injustice within the parent-child relationship so heavy that it produces an injustice in the husband-wife relationship. It is the violation of the commandment "Honor your father and your mother," producing the violation of the commandment "Thou shalt not commit adultery."

Theologically speaking, when we are dealing with the issue of sin in a person's life, does it really make a difference which of God's commands is being violated? When we are looking at the brokenness of a human life, where is the justification to say either the prostitute, or the drug addict, or the liar, or the thief is "better" than the others?

We are dealing with broken lives. There is not much benefit in attempting to determine levels of guilt. We are not entitled to become the instrument of justice and judgment in the place of God. We have been called to be ministers of reconciliation, to the job of healing, not of adding to the hurt. Art already felt guilty and had experienced pain, which no one who has not been in his place can fully appreciate. He needed answers to life and help in restoring his relationships to wholeness rather than condemnation that he had made a mess of things.

The paramount question for couples who face the affair in their relationship is not "How wrong was it?" but rather "What do we now want to do with what we have?" Art expressed his sense of confusion. It would have been unrealistic for him to simply forget about the person with whom he had the affair. They had shared at some level of mutual investment, whether rightly or wrongly, and there necessarily grew from that a measure of indebtedness. He was not free to simply "stop caring." On the other hand, he had made a covenant with his wife, felt responsibility as well as love for her, but also was very guilty.

I am decidedly in favor of marriage because I am strongly convinced that we have little in life of value if we cannot trust one another, and marriage is a covenant of such trust. No one can deny, however, that only those who have made the covenant can decide whether or not they are willing to work to keep it alive. A therapist cannot do for a couple what they are not willing to do for themselves. Even God doesn't impose his will on us in that way. Art and Susan had to decide for themselves whether they would press ahead with one another, or whether the issues of betrayal, guilt, shame, and forgiveness were more than they were ready to handle.

Susan wanted Art back. I warned her that she would later have many disturbing feelings should she and Art get back together. But she still wanted to press for reconciliation. Art decided that he had a much larger investment in Susan than in his friend. He would need fourteen more years of knowing this "other woman" to even begin to compare their life together as a couple to his and Susan's married life together. Art did not want reconciliation just for the sake of the children, nor did Susan want him to, but the children were also an investment Art had to weigh in his decision.

In working toward healing, we went back through their respective family systems. Art began to speak of the hurt he had carried inside for years in response to his father's abandoning him and his mother. He spoke of times early on when he had lain in bed praying that his father would come home, and then, later, in his anger, praying that his father would die, and, still later, seeing himself so caught, praying that he himself would die.

Susan had never known. She had thought that her husband had worked through the anger and hurt over his father years before. She assumed Art was satisfied with his relationship with his father as it was now. She began to understand how Art's getting along well with her father was disloyalty to his own father. She could understand how the frequent visits she, Art, and the kids made to her parents and the relationship the children shared with her parents must have hurt Art.

I encouraged Art to press in on developing his relationship with both his parents. It was difficult for him to do, but Art eventually got together with his father. As they spoke, Art learned of his father's home life with his parents. Art discovered that his grandfather had passed away when his father was in his early teens. And although his father and grandfather had never gotten along well, when grandfather died, he felt a sense of abandonment. His mother and the children were left in unfortunate economic circumstances, and he could not finish school because of the need for added income. Art's father described many of the same feelings Art had gone through. When Art related this to his father, they both began to

laugh, and their laughter provided a comforting sense
of release from the many years of pain.

However, things did not instantly fall into place for Art
and his father. Years of strained relationship had to be
overcome and that process moves slowly. But this was a
beginning. Something had changed for both of them when
Art worked up the courage to place his feelings and his
truth before his father. This was something Art's father had
never had the opportunity to do with his own father, but
through the experience of sharing feelings with his son,
he became somewhat liberated. He began to feel that if
his father had lived long enough, they too would have
reached some level of understanding as he and his son
were now doing.

Dealing with his mother was somewhat different for Art,
and yet somewhat the same. His act of infidelity, although
loyal to his father was extremely disloyal to her. His mother
had always been the strong parent for Art. He always
knew his father would let him get away with more than
she would. Art could connect with feelings inside that he
was still somewhat afraid of his mother. The fear he
experienced was not like that when he would run from
the spanking with a hair brush, but rather like the fear
he had when seeing displeasure on his mother's face.

His mother was invited to come into the sessions. She
was made to understand that Art and Susan were working
on strengthening their marriage and that she could offer
them help. The topic of the affair was not brought up
because it was a symptom, not a cause, and could prove
embarrassing for all concerned. Instead, Art began to talk
of feelings he had had when at home with his mother. He
told how many times he feared that failing to live up to her
standards would cause her to stop loving him. He told her
how important her love and approval had been to him
and how important they still were.

Tears came to her eyes. When she spoke, her words
came out with difficulty, between sobs. She assured Art

that nothing he could do could ever turn her love from him. She said that, as he was growing up, her desire was to direct him to what seemed best for him. Even when he had disobeyed and she had punished him, she still had felt proud to have him as her son. She felt proud now. They were sitting side by side in the therapy room. Art leaned over, hugged her, and thanked her. His mother did not realize why he was thanking her but within those tears and that affirmation of her unconditional love, she had given him permission to be himself. With that came permission to trust his wife more deeply, to pursue a deeper relationship with his father, to make mistakes in life, and then to get back up on his feet and still feel that he was okay.

He was able to talk to his mother about his having gotten closer to his father and to assure her that the relationship he and his mother shared had not diminished in value for him. To his surprise, much of the bitterness he had sensed in her toward his father in times past was not there now. He didn't know whether he had misread her or whether time had softened her feelings. But the reason didn't really matter. He was free to love, without any feeling of guilt, both his mother and his father.

Developing trust with Susan was a distinct issue in itself. Susan spoke of her family as being rather ordinary. Everyone did what he or she was supposed to because it was expected. In her family people avoided conflict or troublesome topics. She had carried this approach into her relationship with Art. It made for peace between them, and she had settled for that instead of truth. So she did not reach out to try to understand Art. She simply assumed everything was all right for him because everything seemed all right for her.

Now, however, there was something undeniable to overcome. He had violated her trust. She expressed that his having sex with another woman was not as painful as his hiding a piece of his life from her. He had been more open to someone else than he had been with her. But she now knew that his silence had its mate in her unwillingness to deal with reality. Their complementary fears were something else that together they would have to work through.

Susan and Art were able to move beyond the problem areas in their relationship to rediscover the value in their life together. Getting past the affair is possible—for couples who choose to do so. It isn't easy and it isn't quick. This brief narrative of one family presents only the highlights of the problems to be faced and the cures to be achieved. Art and Susan spent the better part of a year working through the crisis in their lives, but they felt the effort was worth making. Their success with this very difficult problem holds out hope to multitudes of other broken families who face the problem of the affair.

As serious a violation as sexual infidelity can be, in itself it is not the true obstacle for many couples who are trying to get their lives back together. The real obstacle is the lack of faithfulness manifested in a couple's daily life—the unfaithfulness of not being sensitive to one another; the unfaithfulness of valuing a job or even the children more than one's spouse; the unfaithfulness of not being able to trust, and then, when trust is broken, of not being able to forgive. These are the unfaithfulnesses that violate, at foundational levels, the covenant that reads "till death us do part."

TWELVE
ABOUT DIVORCE
Relational Realignment

A tear glistened at the corner of his eye. He heard the pastor say, "Who gives this woman to be married to this man?" It was hard to get the words past the heavy spot in his throat, but he managed to place his daughter's hand in the hand of her husband-to-be and respond, "Her mother and I."

As he took his seat, his head spun with a confusion of feelings. Few noticed his body heaving slightly with his sobs: "God, she looks beautiful. There's a sparkle of happiness in her eyes I've never seen there before. But she seems so young. Is this really the best thing for her? Will he be as good to her five, ten, fifteen years from now as he has been this past year and a half?" He knew he had tried his best and that from here on she had to decide what to do with her life.

The bride and groom stood staring into each other's eyes. Their thoughts were parallel. They each felt the weight of the step they were taking: ". . . to be my wedded wife, to have and to hold, from this day forward."

The groom had waited long for this day. All the other women he had dated had never evoked from him the

feelings he had for her. He wanted to be her husband.
"For better, for worse, for richer, for poorer . . . ." Life
with her would be wonderful. She was the answer to his
hopes and dreams. She had no equal. " . . .to love and
to cherish, till death us do part . . . ."

There would be children, two or three; she hadn't
decided for sure just how many. They would be like him.
Gentle, caring, but strong and assured. He had made her
life. When they started going together, she discovered a
happiness she had never before known. "He loves me."
The feeling was warm and secure, and she knew it was
true. She knew there would never be anyone else for
either of them. ". . . with this ring I thee wed, in the name of
the Father, and of the Son, and of the Holy Spirit. Amen."

They kissed. Both felt a sense of heaven enveloping
them. They had covenanted together to share their lives in
the most intimate and full way humans can. Their marriage
would last a lifetime. They were sure.

The above is a typical scene, one that takes place week
after week in churches everywhere. We in the congregation
stand as witnesses to the covenant of marriage. We support
the decision of the bridal pair and believe their union will last.

In these times however, what began in church will often
end in the courtroom. The "ceremony" here is a painful
one. Presiding over a dead union, the court divides
responsibility between the former partners. They agreed to
this death ceremony because they saw the effects of their
dying relationship touch each other and the children. Both
knew the marriage had to end before everyone in the
family was irreparably damaged, if not physically, at the
very least, emotionally.

Nevertheless, everyone is in pain. The children know
that they will not be able to grow up with both mother and
father. They will have to choose between them. But they
can hardly be expected to make a decision that is tough
even for adults. The parents are not happy. Each now has
a more difficult financial situation. More significantly, each

now experiences, and will continue for a while to experience in even greater measure, the burdens of failure and guilt. The former partners, despite making excuses, have glimpses of the destruction they fed into the relationship. They realize that the struggle in the marriage for personal dignity and justice was a dirty business, and that hurt was thrown back and forth without measure. They know that in the scheme of their lives, their marriage is one of their most significant failures, perhaps their greatest. They may not be able to discover the reasons or understand why their marriage broke apart, but both experience a deep sense of failure and guilt for their share in its failure.

In unprecedented numbers homes are coming apart. Nothing we have been able to do has seemed to stop this acceleration or even to slow it down. The Church, which has been called by God to the ministry of reconciliation, has not been able to offer much help in understanding how to make the best of what is, to say the least, already a bad situation. If the Church is to move in the vanguard of healing in the lives of our families, we need to reevaluate our response to divorce. Somehow we need to encourage people whose families come apart to press on to wholeness. Granted, there are difficulties (which result from that broken marriage), that they will have to deal with over a prolonged period of time, but they should not have to live out the remainder of life with, as it were, the mark of Cain upon them.

Ginger's mother died when she was ten years old. As the oldest of three children, Ginger was given a large portion of the responsibility to parent the younger children. It was hard, but there were benefits also. She alone, of all the children, got to decide who did what. Dad backed her up and would punish any of the children who failed to obey her. She liked the feeling of authority and was willing to sacrifice some of her childhood for it, at least at that time in her life.

At age seventeen, she no longer felt the thrill of parenting the younger children, but instead wanted more time for herself. She struggled to get it. Her father felt very comfortable with her oversight in the home and didn't want to let her go.

Ginger was very popular at school. Her sense of leadership made her confident in her relationships with her peers, and, being attractive, she had several fellows interested in going out with her. Eventually she became exclusively interested in one boy. Because of the pressures Ginger experienced at home, their relationship mostly grew during the time they were at school. Their dating was limited to weekends and they quickly came to feel they wanted more.

Ginger became pregnant, and even though there was a nasty scene about it at home, it became the leverage that enabled her to pry herself away from the family. Her father, not wanting to deal with the social disgrace of having a child in the home born out of wedlock, consented to her marrying Joe.

Joe was a drug abuser. He was not addicted, but was regularly involved in getting high. Ginger knew about his involvement, although not all of it. She didn't like it when he was high, for then they would usually fight. She persuaded herself that once they were married, she would be able to get him to stop. Of course, her plans did not work out.

Joe had a regular job but he supplemented his income by periodically dealing drugs. Their life was relatively calm until the baby was born. Ginger began to notice that Joe was getting high much more frequently. They were now fighting more and more, and not just with words, but with fists as well. Invariably, Ginger received the worst in these battles.

However, Ginger refused to go home to her father, lest she live with a feeling of the eternal "I told you so." Her friends could do little or nothing to help, and, in fact, as the situation worsened between her and Joe, her friends began to back away. In desperation, Ginger, while watching a religious TV program, gave herself to God. She was put in touch with a local church and began participating regularly in their programs.

At home, the situation continued to worsen. Joe didn't like Ginger's involvement in the church, and, probably as a protest, he became more open with his drug abuse. He even began taking friends home to get high with him. They would inject themselves with needles in front of both Ginger and her daughter, who was now a toddler. Ginger lived constantly in fear that these scenes would produce emotional damage to her child, and that the police would break in and raid her home.

Ginger was encouraged by the people at the church. They told her to hold on and to keep praying for her husband and that God would work things out. She prayed and she prayed. For two years she waited for things to get better. They didn't. She decided to leave Joe and try to provide a decent home for their daughter.

Joe tried to get back with her at first, but only on his terms, that he would still have drugs as a part of his life. When Ginger refused, he cut off contact. He neither contributed support to his daughter, nor ever tried to visit with her. As a matter of fact, after a while, Ginger didn't know where he was or even how to get in touch with him.

Life can become very lonely with no one but a child to be intimate with. Ginger came to me as a person in a mild depression. She was crying a lot, sometimes snapping at her daughter for nothing, and wanting to spend more and more time sleeping.

When the issue of loneliness came up, I asked Ginger if she dated at all. She was still young and attractive; it was hard to imagine that she would not have had offers. She said she didn't date because she was still married and didn't know if, as a Christian, she was allowed to remarry. She wasn't interested in getting into a male-female relationship that would only end in frustration. I pressed a little harder to find out if there was anything else bothering her. There was. She was afraid that even if she were free to get married, she might end up getting hurt all over again. She did not want to fail at marriage twice.

Several issues needed to be raised. What still remained between her and Joe needed to be reworked: Feelings of love, hurt, and anger; feelings about him as a person. And even if Ginger never wanted to see him again, her child might. He could not simply be dismissed as though he had never existed.

There was the question of a broken covenant. It was easy to see how Joe had failed at his responsibility (especially since Joe wasn't there to speak for himself), but what was Ginger's part? What part did she play in breaking up what is supposed to be one of life's strongest support relationships? She readily admitted that she hadn't been the perfect wife (what wife is) but it seemed difficult for her to get down to specifics. Some of the things that eventually came up were that she was sometimes spiteful in her actions, and that she emotionally drew away from him and toward her daughter as they began to have more serious problems. She failed to be supportive of him in his struggle with drugs. She instead tried to mother him, to tell him what he had to do. It is clear that the covenant breaks from both sides. Although one is perhaps more guilty than the other, there is no innocent party.

Another area that needed inquiry was her relationship with her father. Ginger admitted that she had wanted to escape from home when she became pregnant. Perhaps subconsciously the pregnancy was not an accident, but a convenient circumstance; she didn't know for sure. At the time she had been aware of birth control methods and had known the possible consequences when they were not used. Eventually, Ginger came to feel she had manipulated Joe into marrying her when she had found she was pregnant. With a mixture of mild guilt and an appeal to his manhood, she had led the way to the altar. In doing so, she had abandoned her father, leaving him alone to finish raising the other children.

The fact that she hardly ever visited her father and he never came to her home informed me that there was definitely unfinished business between them. If Ginger wanted to reduce her chances of relational failure in the future, she was going to have to reconnect with her father and open up dialogue that would help her to know where he was and why he had done what he had done as well as tell her side to him. To do this would require a clearer thinking through on her part as to what she had been feeling in the past at home and what she was feeling now.

Finally, we got to the issue of the rightness or wrongness of divorce as a Christian. I shared with Ginger that I was raised to believe that divorce was wrong and that I still believe it is wrong. But the implications of divorce, like the implications of many Christian standards, are not cut and dried. The issue is not whether or not divorce is wrong; the issue is whether or not that wrong can be forgiven. Can a divorced and remarried person be a 100 percent Christian, or must he or she remain in a second class status?

This issue is certainly a weighty one and cannot be brushed off lightly by those of us who are faced with dealing with broken homes day after day. Following are some of my reflections on the matter.

The Covenant Between God and Man

In the Old Testament, God made a covenant with Abraham and, by extension, with the future nation of Israel. He promised to provide blessing and prosperity if Abraham and the people followed his instructions. God remained faithful to the covenant. When Israel followed his instructions, they prospered; when the people drifted away from him, they suffered.

In reality the covenant was made unilaterally, because

God knew that man could promise but never guarantee—
only he, God, can guarantee the future. The covenant
takes place within the setting of the law—a law
so complete that it discloses the imperfections of each of
us. And it punishes those imperfections severely, exacting
the prescribed eye for an eye and tooth for a tooth.

The law condemned to death anyone who cursed or
struck his father or mother. The law condemned witches
and idolaters to death. Under the law a man who was
found gathering sticks on the Sabbath was taken outside
the camp and stoned.

The richness of the gospel of Jesus Christ is that Jesus
reconciled man to God through grace. Because of Jesus,
those who were indebted to the law were forgiven. The
Spirit of God loved man into a place of freedom and
liberty. Man was given a new birth, a new beginning,
another chance to start clean. God's response to the
broken covenant was to work out a program whereby
those who experienced failure might have a chance to
experience success within a new covenant.

Marriage as a Covenant

There can be no question for the Bible student that
marriage partakes of the nature of the relationship between
God and man. In the Old Testament, Israel is referred to
as the unfaithful wife, and in the New Testament we read
of the Church as the "Bride of Christ."

Certainly God intends human marriage to be a
relationship of faithfulness that would endure until death.
When Jesus was questioned about the legality of divorce,
he expressed that Moses had allowed it because of the
hardness of their hearts. "But," he went on to say, "from
the beginning of the creation God made them male and
female. For this cause shall a man leave his father and
mother, and cleave to his wife; and they twain shall be
one flesh: so then they are no more twain, but one flesh.

What therefore God hath joined together, let not man put asunder" (Mark 10:6-9). He went on to say that divorce and remarriage constitute adultery, which is a sin numbered among the ten commandments. We are made aware that God leaves no latitude for diminishing the value and the strength of the covenant of marriage. The implication is that marriage is not only a covenant between a man and a woman, but also one that is between them and God.

The Issue of Sin and Forgiveness

Divorce is a violation of the covenant. Any violation constitutes "sin," or, as it is more literally translated from the Scriptures, "missing the mark." In an average lifetime we "miss the mark" at least a thousand times, probably more.

However, many of us view the sin of divorce differently from the way we view multitudes of other failures. Many Christians see divorce as a violation that can never be forgiven—or so it seems to the millions of divorced persons who have tried to hold on to their faith in the midst of their traumatic experience. It seems easier for an alcoholic or a thief to be accepted into the church as whole, than for a divorced person. The alcoholic and the thief can repent and begin a new life. The divorced person is charged to go back to the problems of his or her old life and to live with these problems. In this area, many in the Church seem to have forgotten the message of God's grace, that he provides means for redemption from brokenness.

I would raise three questions at this point that may be of help in seeing some options for the redemption of divorced people. First, when Jesus speaks of those who divorce and remarry as committing adultery, was he speaking only of a sexual act, or was he also referring to a violation of faithfulness within a committed relationship? There seems to be a basis to hear Jesus dealing, as he often did with the Pharisees, with the issue of what is legal as opposed to what is spiritual. We might then understand him to be saying, "It is because of the weakness of your humanity that Moses gave you legal permission to dissolve a marriage covenant, but don't fail to understand that that is not the spirit of the covenant, and it constitutes a sin of unfaithfulness when it is exercised."

The second question I would raise is whether we can see unfaithfulness in the marriage before the marriage ends and before the marriage partners divorce and remarry. Isn't there a bit of adultery in the husband who marries his career and puts professional considerations before his wife and children? Isn't there some adultery in the wife who talks out her problems with her mother instead of communicating with her husband? Wasn't there adultery in Joe's marriage to drug abuse?

My years of experience in marriage and family counseling have led me to believe that in most cases John and Jane Doe have beat their love to death with their own brands of unfaithfulness. One particularly unfortunate and common brand of unfaithfulness is emotional incest, the pairing up of one parent and the child (or children) against the other parent. I have found sexual unfaithfulness, what is commonly understood as "adultery," is only a symptom— the tip of the iceberg of relational abandonment and failure. Divorce, in most families, is simply the closure of a relationship that has been dead and laid to rest years before.

Is there a place where a divorced person can pick up the pieces and reestablish a whole relationship with God? If the stories of the Bible are given to expand our understanding of God's principles, we find some basis to believe reconciliation can be found for those who divorce. In the narrative of David and Bathsheba, we are confronted with adultery and then with a murder. The first child of their union died even after David had repented. However, following this, not only did God leave David and Bathsheba's relationship intact, he also blessed it with

Solomon, who later became the next king and a man
in touch with God.

The story seems to present us with an interesting choice
of interpretations: Either we make opportunity for
repentance for an unfaithful relationship, or we allow for
the murder of the extra person (the husband or wife) and
then forgive both the murder and the adultery! I do not
mean to be facetious. I want to press home the fact that
unless we can offer some clear solutions to the destroyed
families, we are missing the cues from God. God seems
to be consistent in making an offer for forgiveness and
restoration upon the confession and repentance of the
one who failed. Some of the consequences for past
mistakes aren't removed, but forgiveness is offered to
the one who fails.

If I am forced to choose between the possibility of erring
on the side of legalism or erring on the side of grace, I will
choose the side of grace. Ginger's path led her through a
divorce with Joe (who, in any event wasn't interested in
reconciliation) and into a new marriage in which she is
finding fulfillment in what it means to be one flesh.

I would like to make some suggestions to pastors and
church leaders which might better prepare them in the
generations to come to meet not only those who are
divorced, but to minister in love to the children of those
marriages who may be desperately in need of inner healing.

We might begin by recognizing that as Christians we
are interested in integrity in our relationship with God.
God has established that the union of man and woman is
sacred. His desire is that we deal with it as such. I have
had couples come into the counseling room speaking of
divorce, but who, in reality, simply didn't know how to
work through their hurts and conflicts. They still loved
one another and were still strong enough to work at
reconciliation. Years later I have seen these same
couples happier than they ever were before.

I wish all family problems could move in the direction

of reconciliation, but some cannot. I have seen couples who have dropped enough explosives on their relationship to overkill it ten times, and even when the relationship is over, they still struggle. They don't have the strength or the resources to remain married any longer. They have destroyed all basis for relational trustworthiness and no inner healing can begin until they separate.

Let us be diligent in encouraging couples to seek out good professional help at the first signs of trouble. Let us not be guilty of dismissing something serious with a prayer and a pat on the back because we are afraid to acknowledge that a problem is beyond our expertise. Let us attempt to do what preventive work we can by teaching people how to love and to communicate within a family system. But when a marriage covenant fails, and there is no hope or promise of reconciliation, let us support a man and woman in realigning their covenant so that they can redeem their integrity and dignity out of their failure.

THIRTEEN
THE WICKED STEPPARENT
No Substitute for Real Parents

"You're not my daddy, and I don't love you."
These words, often repeated, convinced Mike and Rita
they needed help with their family. Little Renee, now six
years old, would make that pronouncement each time she
was in conflict with Mike. Mike would become frustrated
and withdraw from his wife, Rita, as he inevitably
transferred his anger from the child to her mother.

When finally they would discuss the situation, Mike
would say that he had trouble loving Renee because,
although he wanted to love her, it was sometimes very
hard because the child pulled away. Rita, in turn, would
become angry at Mike. She believed that he might be
deliberately trying to create problems within the family.
By the end of their "honest communication," both Mike
and Rita felt they were further apart than ever.

Behind this family's dilemma lay much sadness. Mike
had been married before. He and his wife had two
children, a boy and a girl. Mike had a job that frequently
took him away from the home for a week or two at a time.
His wife often had expressed to him her unhappiness with

this arrangement and her willingness to live on less money in order to have him at home more often. To Mike, his job was his security, and he wasn't about to give it up.

If Mike or his wife had been asked at that time if they loved each other, both would have said yes. In their opinion, their marrige was experiencing stress because of their situation, not because of an absence of love. That was not to last long. Mike began sensing trouble in the relationship when, after returning from a two-week trip, his wife behaved distantly toward him. On the surface, she went through the motions of their life together. They hugged and kissed at the door. She prepared a meal for him. After the children went to bed, she made coffee and they sat watching TV together snuggled up on the sofa. They closed out the night by making love. Mike said he felt as if she had covered herself with a lace net. He could touch and talk to her, but he was conscious of something between them.

Things seemed to improve during the next three weeks while he was at home. But when, after another week away, Mike returned, lace had turned to steel, and he could not reach through. He was met this time without the hug and kiss. His wife informed him that the children were at her mother's home because she had to talk to him about something very important. She felt she owed him an explanation, and, as hard as it was for her to do, she would face him to say she was leaving. She had developed an interest in someone else while he was away. Even though she was not prepared to make any commitment to this new love, she had discovered that she didn't feel any love for Mike, and hadn't for a while. She felt it was better to separate than to take the children through the ugliness that would develop if they continued to live together.

It was a unilateral decision. Mike had no choice. Two willing partners are needed to form a marriage, but only one to take it apart. Mike was not a fighter. He asked only that he be permitted regular visiting times with his children,

a request his wife was happy to arrange. Though accepting
it passively, Mike was hurt by the separation. He started
drinking heavily, to the point where he lost interest in
almost everything and began to be tardy and careless at
work. The first time his boss confronted him, Mike quit,
rather than face the threat of being fired. He then went on
public assistance for about a year, doing little except
allowing time to slide by. It was during this period that he
met Rita. Rita changed his life.

Rita had come to the same place as he had, but by a
different route. She and her husband had been married
about four years when Renee was born. They had both
been employed up to that time and had developed a
very comfortable and financially secure life-style. People
described theirs as the "ideal marriage." They both made
a fuss over Renee, shared in her care, always did things
as a family, and rarely argued and then not for long.

One afternoon, while Renee slept in her crib upstairs,
Rita was raped on the living room floor. A man from the
neighborhood whom Rita did not know, but who
apparently knew that Rita was home alone each afternoon,
knocked at the door, asking for water to cool down his car.
Rita closed the front door, but did not lock it, and started
toward the kitchen. Instantly the man was in the house.
He grabbed her from behind and, with a knife, threatened
her and the baby if she didn't cooperate.

This event happened before groups like Women
Organized Against Rape began to make an impact on the
police and the judicial system. Rita was treated almost as
though she had been the rapist rather than the victim.
Although her name was not mentioned in the newspaper
account of the attack, the neighbors had seen the police
cars race up to her home in response to her call for help.
They simply put two and two together when they read the
story in the newspaper. What they also "put together" was
that she had been more cooperative than she said—that
she had been "asking for it."

A traumatic experience such as this invariably puts much stress on a husband-wife relationship. The wounds to their conjugal love, the stress of the legal process, and the pressures of community stigma all began to press the relationship to its limits. Within nine months Rita was alone. Her husband left one day without an explanation. He simply told her he was leaving, and left.

Renee was not yet two years old. Rita did not wish to leave the child in the care of a baby-sitter in order to work. So she decided to go on public assistance until the baby was older. When Rita and Mike met one night at a club, they almost instantly were drawn together. They both had been "left" by their spouses, and had since struggled to ease the pain and make some sense of life.

When, many months later, the question of marriage arose, both Mike and Rita had fears. The decision was a while coming, and Rita says that one of the things she was most concerned about was whether Mike and Renee would get along well. If they could not love each other, she would not go through with the marriage. Both Mike and Renee said they cared very much about one another, and, in fact, Renee even seemed anxious to have her mother marry Mike.

Problems began to arise in our sessions when I asked Rita if Renee ever knew her real father. Rita began to radiate a coldness that could crystalize water. With great indignation she told me that she had met him a few times but only for very brief meetings. When I asked what she had told Renee about her father, she responded that she had told the child the truth—that when Renee was just a little baby, her father had walked out on them. And, although she didn't know why, her father had never tried to get in touch. I began to understand what was happening.

Rita was angry at her ex-husband. No doubt she had reason to be. But her feelings were affecting her daughter and subsequently Mike as well. Rita, in the next several sessions, made it clear that she had passed a death sentence on the relationship between Renee and her father. The rationale was, "He doesn't deserve it." In response to the question of whether or not Renee was entitled to access to her real father, Rita responded, "She doesn't need someone like him."

A decision had been made between Mike and Rita that Mike would now be Renee's father. The only problem was that Renee knew he wasn't. And, in fact, Mike also knew that he wasn't. He still visited regularly with his son and daughter, and found relating to them much easier than to Renee. Out of the triad, only Rita, who loved both Mike and Renee very much couldn't understand why their relationship wasn't good.

It wasn't good because it wasn't based on reality. It simply wasn't true that Mike was Renee's father. Mike could certainly perform many of the functions of a father in the home, but there was an indelible line he could not traverse. He was not her father.

I sometimes find in families a denial of reality so intense that it borders on psychosis. Family members can press so hard to believe what they wish were true that they lose sight of where reality ends and fantasy begins. It seems to me that when we subtly pressure a child to deny that a parent-child relationship really exists, we violate the commandment to honor father and mother. As a churchman, I know that many Christians are far more comfortable dealing with issues in terms of black and white rather than attempting to deal with the areas of gray. It is much easier to put together that father is not at home; stepfather is; he is fulfilling the responsibilities of a father; therefore, he is the true father.

I would suggest a different approach, an approach that would keep the child in touch with reality. The real father should be acknowledged as father, and the stepfather recognized as the man responsible for fulfilling the male role in the home. The facts of the separation should be explained to the child when the child is ready to hear them. For example, a child of four might ask, "Mommy, where is my daddy?" The mother might answer, "I don't know, Honey. Daddy went away a long time ago and didn't say where he was going." That child might not ask another "daddy question" for a year, and so there would then be no need to raise the issue. Would it be at all helpful to this child to say, "Daddy didn't love us, so he went away and never gets in touch?" This may help the mother to ventilate some of her angry feelings, and it may serve to fuse the child more securely to the mother, but it doesn't seem to be of any help to the child.

When either parent attempts to answer the questions of a child about the other parent, there has to be a distortion. I can tell my children only what I think their mother felt when she said or did a certain thing. No one can know for sure what another person is thinking or feeling. I am much closer to the truth when I say to my child, "I don't know why your mother did that; only she can tell you." The child, in fact, may never get an answer, if the other parent chooses to be silent. But who of us gets an answer to all we wish to know? Children, like all of us, need to learn sometime in life to accept both the "no answer" answer and the "I don't know" answer. They will either learn to handle them, or they will try to sort out in confusion "the truth" from what you or I thought was the truth, and in the process learn to distrust us.

Several things must be said concerning the other parent who has left. It may be difficult for many of us to understand the phenomenon of leaving one's children, but it is commonly done. Usually a person does not leave his children; he leaves his spouse. The children are caught in the middle, forced to live with one parent or the other because they cannot be divided into equal shares. A parent's leaving should not be interpreted as a message that he or she does not love the children, but rather of having difficulty coping with things as they are in the home. He or she believes that leaving is necessary. This is not to say the move is good, but that the absent parent is following what is seen as the only viable alternative at the time.

We must accept the fact that people can change. Mike went through a change after his wife left. The job he would not consider changing while they were together, he gave up when his family broke up. He drank heavily until he met Rita, then stopped and went back to work, in a different field, when there was a need to do so. Perhaps the move away from home is a mistake. Perhaps in his, or her, confusion a person makes a decision at a certain point in time that separates him from those who may very well be the most important people in his life, his children. Does that decision mean that a person is never again entitled to reconnect with his child, admit his mistake, and go on to rebuild something than can be meaningful to both parent and child?

Also, whose decision should it be as to how a child feels about a parent who has left? Isn't the child entitled to deal with the relationship on the basis of what he chooses to do with it? Perhaps the relationship will never work out. I would simply argue for the right of the child to discover this fact without the influence or interference of the parent with whom he lives. Renee's attitude will not simply go away. Chances are much greater that as she gets older, she will fight the imposed notion of Mike's being her father with even greater vigor.

Rita had to come to grips with another reality. She seemed to think that children are automatically lovable, that because Renee was only six years old, Mike should be magnetically drawn to her. Nothing could be further from the truth. Of course, little children have a vulnerability that draws from us a protective instinct, and in their smallness they are physically appealing. Also, by virtue of their moving in a different realm from ours, they become nonthreatening and so we can draw closer to them more

quickly than we can to adults. But if by love we mean that
we become willing to make a commitment to fight through
life together, to work out the conflicts with a sense of
integrity, to stand together through thick and thin, then
I would respond that loving a child is not automatic.

All of us have met children who have rubbed us the
wrong way from the start. Our responses have ranged from
the kindly "I find him somewhat difficult" to the gut-level
"I could wring his neck." These are children we have no
desire to be with, much less work through problems with
them. The more responsible we are forced to be for their
behavior, by virtue of being a baby sitter, school teacher,
or stepparent, the more resentful we become. Outwardly,
we may appear unruffled, but each day our feelings are
newly wounded.

In cases such as Rita and Mike's, the stepparent and
child are competing for first place in the other parent's life.
Both want to be more special than the other, and both are
entitled to be so, but for different reasons. Renee is Rita's
daughter. Without question, Rita has a great responsibility
in that relationship. On the other hand, Mike is Rita's
chosen mate. The marriage covenant includes the words
". . . and forsaking all others, keep thee only unto
him. . . ." Therefore, it precludes a divided allegiance on
Rita's part. The problem is, however, that this family
situation itself is one of divided allegiance. In addition to
the dilemma of which relationship has priority, there is the
dilemma of parenting the child.

In a home where the child lives with both natural
parents, any problem is fair game for either parent to deal
with. When discipline is called for, the child is able to work
through to forgiveness of the "offending" parent. However,
in the case of the stepparent, the child does not feel
obligated to forgive. Also, the natural parent of the child
may wonder whether or not the stepparent is being as fair
to the child as he would be to his own natural child. At
times the stepparent himself questions his ability to be fair.

The dilemma of parenting in such a household is that, on one hand, parenting by only the natural parent is not helpful to the child, and, on the other, shared parenting by the natural and the stepparent can cause serious problems.

In such a situation, we cannot expect that the desired quality of family will be achieved. That achievement is precluded by the tragedy of two broken family systems coming together to make a new unit. Mike and Rita must work with Renee to do the best they can with the resources they have available. Rita needs to understand that the conflict between Mike and Renee is different from any conflict between her and Renee. Mike has to understand the unnaturalness of trying to raise a child whose father in fact he is not. He has to be able to accept the naturalness of his inner vacillation. Both Mike and Rita have to explore the possibilities of establishing some relationship with Renee's father, possibly by bringing Renee in touch with her grandparents on that side of the family. The grandparents' relationship to their son will give some balance to Rita's projection of her former husband and enable Renee to better understand this man, who, for better or worse, is her father.

The truth is that we cannot change blood relationships. Marriage is a relationship of choice. We select a person whom we marry, and we can divorce that person at a later point and end the relationship. The parent-child relationship is one of fact—not choice. We cannot erase the lines that connect parent and child. They are there whether we acknowledge them or not. There is, however, no law that says that people other than the natural mother and father cannot be very helpful to a child by being involved in the child's parenting. Children, as a rule, do not resent the discipline of an aunt, uncle, grandparent, or even older cousin if it is subject to the authority of the parents. Children such as Renee could be helped greatly if they were made to understand that even though the stepparent is not the real parent, he is in charge of them, and whether they love him or not, they have to obey him while they are living with him. Granted, it takes strength on the part of both parent and stepparent to go this route, but if they can, it will strengthen the relationships within their home.

FOURTEEN
THE SINGLE-PARENT HOME
Filling in the Blank

Death is an expected transformation for the elderly, often coming as God's gift of liberation from pain, immobility, and the effects of mental fatigue. When, however, death takes a man in his late thirties, whether by a fatal accident or by a terminal illness, we feel a deep sense of tragedy because, in our view of things, someone that young is not supposed to die.

Real life doesn't move according to the fairy tale description, where everyone lives happily ever after. Real life is packed with tragedy and those of us who experience the death of a young spouse can only pick up the pieces and keep moving on. Harriet was in this situation when Phil died and left her alone with two small children to raise.

As a child, Harriet had always been happy. She seemed almost to float through life. She had been born on a farm. Her parents were not poor but neither was their farm a large operation. The family lived well, the children daily carrying out appointed chores, and the parents pulling together to run the farm. Harriet, as a little girl, had talked about becoming a nurse, and when high school graduation was accomplished, her parents willingly paid the tuition so Harriet could fulfill her dream.

In spite of the professional training that tells a nurse not to become emotionally involved with her patients, Harriet found Phil very attractive when he was in for two weeks of testing and treatment. Phil had regularly asked for her phone number. At first she had tried to remain aloof, but later gave in to his request. She would not have forgiven herself if he, after being discharged, didn't know how to contact her. They married shortly after her graduation from nursing school, and they moved to a city many miles from her home town. Phil didn't have family in the new town either. They were there only because his company had transferred him. He knew that if he wanted to succeed, he would have to move to wherever the company wanted him, so over the next ten years, they moved several times.

Harriet was doing well. She had left nursing for a couple of years in order to have her children. When they were old enough for a day-care center, she returned to work. She was always able to find work wherever Phil was transferred, and since she enjoyed both her family and her work, she was happy.

Then, suddenly, it happened. One day at work she received a call that Phil had become sick on the job. She was told nothing more except which hospital he had been taken to. Harriet immediately called the hospital and was informed that her husband had been rushed into the cardiac care unit. Immediately she signed out, and drove across town to the other hospital. There, a doctor told her that her husband was already dead. The medics had done all they could, but Phil simply had not responded, and they had lost him.

She was stunned. She sat for a long while in the reception room trying to clear her mind as well as her eyes. She saw people die all the time, but this time it was Phil. She had never let herself think about Phil dying, but it had happened nonetheless. She asked to see the body.

Perhaps in the recesses of her mind was the hope that somehow the doctors were wrong. The heart monitor unit might be broken. Perhaps Phil's heart had spontaneously recovered. She looked for anything that would turn this nightmare into a benign dream. But when she saw Phil's body, she knew definitely that he was dead. The chapter of marriage in Harriet's life had ended. Once again she was a single woman, and the chapters ahead also would carry much pain.

How does one begin to explain when the smiling faces of her two children come through the door with the usual "Hi, Mom. Anything to eat?" What Harriet had to tell them would bury their appetites and, surely for a time, their spirits as under an avalanche of grief. Harriet could not be sure which was the greater pain—the loss of her husband, or the suffering through the children's pain as they began to realize they had lost their father. We believers speak of a soul at peace. Through the death of a loved one we attempt to focus on the presence of God. But in the depths of our being is a terrible wail that continues to echo in the emptiness that is us.

Harriet did not remarry. She was able to support her family on the money she earned, so she was not under economic pressure. She still had strong feelings about her relationship with Phil and didn't want to get caught in a relationship that might not be as good. She was fearful of subjecting her children to an adoptive father and possibly adding to their discomfort in life. These reasons were the ones she gave for not remarrying. I suspect that stronger than any was the unspoken one: If she married again, this man too might die and leave her once more with the pain of loss.

When her son, Jeff, was twelve, Harriet became concerned. He was getting into trouble at school, having problems with some of the adults at church, and had started to spend his spare time with youngsters that, like him, had reputations as troublemakers. When Harriet went to school, the counselor told her that Jeff seemed to be harboring something deep within that he was unwilling to talk about with others. It most likely had to do with his father's death. Two incidents seemed to point in this direction. Once in a discussion at school, Jeff, in mentioning something about a project his father had been working at, spoke as though his father were still alive. The second incident was a fight Jeff had been involved in that seemed to be provoked by nothing more than another boy's bragging about his own father. These occurrences suggested that Harriet take him to someone for professional help.

I spoke with the whole family. Harriet explained why they had come. I asked Jeff if he saw things as his mother did or if he had a different view. He was abrupt and withdrawn. He simply shrugged his shoulders and said, "I don't know."

Jeff's sister was two years younger than he. She seemed very well adjusted and spoke very freely. "Jeff seems to be going through a change. He acts different. He didn't used to be so mean."

I discovered that it had been four years since his father had died. Jeff had been only eight years old and had had a two-sided relationship with his father. He had loved him a lot and they had done many things together, but Jeff had also been very afraid of him. His father had been a strict disciplinarian. His voice alone had been threatening. I saw that Jeff had some unresolved feelings about his father. As a small child he saw his father as threatening. At times when he would get punished, Jeff had hated him and thought how much better it would be if he were not part of the family. Perhaps once or twice he had even dared to think, "I wish he was dead."

When it happened, Jeff assumed some of the guilt. Maybe his father had died because he had wished him dead. Maybe if he had been a better child, God wouldn't have taken his father. He would have taken someone else's. These are the thoughts that can form in an eight-year-old mind.

In a sense, Jeff was also angry with his father because he had abandoned him. Now he was twelve, and entering puberty. He was on his way to being a man but wasn't even sure what a man was supposed to be. He could not get close to another man because this would be a betrayal of his special love for his father, and because, like his mother, he didn't trust relationships with men because, again, he might be abandoned. Karen, his sister, had her mother to model from. Jeff needed a trustworthy male to which he could relate.

I explored with Harriet what her relationship was like with her parents. She told how, when she and Phil were married, her father had not been pleased. He had made remarks to the effect that the marriage probably wouldn't last long and that she would be running back to him for help. For this reason she had not moved back to where her family still lived.

I asked if she had ever talked to her father about his feelings later in her married life. She said she thought he had accepted the relationship because on holidays her father and Phil seemed to get along tolerably well. But, she had never actually spoken to him about the matter; she had just forgotten about it.

There was obviously something contradictory here. Harriet was saying that she had dismissed her father's remark as no longer valid, but at the same time had said that because of his remark she hadn't moved back to her home town. Hers was a sort of "I'll show him" action. I suggested that she might find it very therapeutic to get in touch with him and talk about his feelings about her marriage both during its beginning as well as at its end. She couldn't see how talking to her father would help Jeff, but she was willing to do it anyway.

We returned to Jeff. After several sessions he had begun to talk. It was important that he rework his relationship with

his dad even though his father was now dead. The
relationship would be reworked in Jeff's understanding
rather than in interaction with his father. I asked Jeff to
go back to an incident in the past where his father had
become angry and punished him. Jeff recounted an
incident that stood out in his mind. We explored how he
had felt at the time. He acknowledged fear, anger, and
paranoia. He didn't know if the incident would affect his
father's attitude toward him. I asked how his father had
afterwards acted. He described doing things again with
him and gradually feeling as though he had forgotten the
incident. But, he went on, "With Dad it was impossible
to know when he might become angry again."

I followed this line of questioning to see if Jeff could
ever remember his father holding a grudge. Had he ever
punished him again weeks after a disobedience or seemed
to be angry with him long afterwards? He thought back.
His recollection of him was that he would get angry and
loud, but get over his anger pretty quickly. Harriet agreed.
Phil wouldn't get upset often, and when he did he was like
a brief thunderstorm that soon allows the sun to come out
again. He didn't carry grudges. They were much more
her thing.

Gradually, Jeff began to see his father differently.
We then dealt with the fact that God, like his father, loved
Jeff and hadn't punished him by taking away his father.
That God, in fact, had used him to punish Jeff when he
had done wrong things so that he would not go through
life continuing to do these wrong things. His father had not
been perfect, but overall, what he had given to his son was
good. Jeff readily accepted this explanation. He had been
much happier with him around even when he had
punished him. We were helping Jeff to develop trust in
both his earthly father and his heavenly Father. But there
was still a need for that ongoing example of manliness that
Jeff could emulate, and the most natural resource was his
grandfather. Jeff could get close to him without any sense

of disloyalty to his father since grandfather was flesh and blood kin.

When summer vacation was nearing, Harriet, at my suggestion, made arrangements to take her children to visit her parents for a week on the farm. During the session before they left, Karen was excited, Jeff was playing urban tough, and Harriet was admittedly nervous. She had kept in contact with her folks regularly by phone and mail, but had never spent this amount of time in her parents' home since her marriage. Both parents had responded with enthusiasm when she had called, but Harriet thought that a week could be a long time, and was unsure of what might happen.

When they returned from vacation, I discovered several things. First of all, they all had survived living under the same roof. Harriet couldn't believe how pleasant it had been for her. She had gone about the house almost with the sense of never having left. So many of her old memories were still there. The kids had had a great time. Everything, even the chores their grandfather assigned to them the first day of their visit had been fun.

One evening toward the end of their visit, as the adults were seated around the kitchen table after supper, Harriet had mentioned how well the kids had taken to the farm. She was shocked to hear her father say, "It might not be a bad idea for you to think about moving back to this area. Your mother and I are getting on in years now, and we would be comfortable having you here with us. The farm would be good for you, too. We had hoped you'd come back when Phil died, but we didn't want you to feel we were trying to run your life."

For years Harriet had believed she couldn't return home. Pride and fear, like barbs pressing into her flesh, had kept her from discussing the issue with her parents. She had cheated herself of two of the best human resources she could have had in going through her grief.

During the week an incident occurred that put his

grandfather in the role of Dad for Jeff. Driving the tractor was the most exciting thing Jeff could imagine. His grandfather allowed him to drive out in the field when they were working there together. Driving the tractor wasn't at all dangerous, because his grandfather sat against the back fender watching every move Jeff made. Seated in the tractor, Jeff couldn't have felt more powerful if he were flying the world's fastest fighter jet. Jeff spent more time working with his grandfather than doing anything else. Whenever Jeff was done with his assigned chores, he would hunt down his grandfather and help him in whatever way he could. As a result, he regularly got to drive the tractor. His grandfather's instructions were that Jeff was not to operate the tractor without supervision, because it was a very powerful machine and someone or something could be hurt.

One evening just after supper, Jeff and Karen had gone out to play. The adults were still at the dinner table when all of a sudden they heard the tractor motor begin to race. Grandfather leaped from the table and ran out to the barn, with Harriet and her mother right behind. Jeff had decided to show off for Karen. She had suggested he didn't really know anything about tractors, and so he had climbed onto the machine and started it up.

Even before his grandfather reached the tractor, he yelled for Jeff to shut it off. Jeff felt the same explosion inside himself that he remembered when his father had gotten angry. He jumped down from the seat and started running away from his grandfather, toward the house. A yell stopped him in his tracks. Calling him back, his grandfather scolded him, saying he had been warned never to touch the tractor when he wasn't around. Now, Jeff would have to go to bed for the rest of the evening, as punishment. Jeff had looked to Harriet for help, but she simply said, "Well, what are you waiting for? Go inside."

Jeff brooded through the next morning. He did his chores, then stayed around the house rather than find his grandfather. At lunchtime, when the family was seated around the table eating, Jeff discovered that his grandfather was treating him as if nothing had happened. He seemed no longer to be angry. That afternoon, the two were working together again. Jeff was learning to develop trust for a male example. His grandfather's trustworthiness was found in his willingness to hold Jeff accountable in a fair way.

It is extremely important for the single parent, whether divorced or widowed, whether male or female, to realize his or her children's need to have significant input from people of the opposite sex. These resource people are often grandparents, who are usually already invested in the children. If grandparents are deceased, as was Jeff's paternal grandfather, aunts and uncles can sometimes become good resources.

Parents need to work together as a team to help their child develop. A single parent, therefore, has to look toward an adult of the opposite sex to help in behavior modeling, structure, and discipline. Harriet's standing with her father in Jeff's punishment was a way of giving grandfather permission to continue to help structure life for Jeff. It also prevented the futile cycle of Jeff's winning over grandfather and thereby losing a trustworthy model of male behavior.

Some single parents feel that their children are already being punished by not having the other parent. They fear that support of someone else's discipline for their child will result in the child's thinking he is being abandoned again. As parents we know we are responsible for the disciplining of our children. However, others can be helpful in this work. I am not suggesting that a grandfather can be a replacement for a father—that simply cannot be the case. But single parents need to develop resources that fill out the parenting picture to help children develop more completely.

FIFTEEN
IDENTIFYING
RESOURCES
Fruit in the Family Tree

For every family the sense of wholeness comes when each member is free to give and receive both from other members of the family as well as from society at large. It is no more healthy when one family member overgives than when he or she overtakes. The same is true for a family unit in its relationship within its community. We should be seeking in both cases a balance.

Because today's family system is affected by the last generation and the generation before, each of us needs to raise the question of what imbalance may have existed in our father's, grandfather's, or even great-grandfather's lives that might be causing an imbalance for us now. We need to research the family tree to identify these areas of imbalance as well as to dig out resources. We may be trying to repay a societal debt of our family system without realizing that one or two other members of our larger family, who like us are unaware of the mutual problem, have been working on that same issue.

For example, look at a hypothetical family, the Quincys. Great-grandfather Quincy was a congressman from his

home state. After many years of service he was found to
be involved in criminal activities, cheating taxpayers out of
money. He was sentenced to a significant prison term and
died shortly after his release. He never had time to reverse
society's feelings about him. One of his two sons became
involved in organized crime, making his father look good
by comparison, and the other son became a country
doctor. After working hard to become a doctor, he
practically gave his life away to repay his father's debt
to society.

In the next generation, the family of the man in the
syndicate produced a plumber, a syndicate man, a school
teacher, and a priest. The doctor's family produced a high-
priced heart specialist, a heroin addict, and a politician
fighting organized crime. Each branch of the family made
efforts to both affirm great-grandfather Quincy as a
worthwhile person, by making his crime seem small, as
well as to repay his debt of dishonesty to society. Yet,
because of geographical distance and lack of extended
family contact, none of the great-grandchildren may be
aware of what members in the other half of the family
have been doing to work on the inherited shame.

In a made-up situation like the Quincy family, we are
exaggerating the flow of behavior from one generation to
the other and are not at all considering the implications of
the family systems of the spouses. In a real family the flow
of action would be a bit more difficult to trace, but usually
can be discovered if we search diligently.

As I work at family therapy, I am amazed to discover
how little people really know about their extended families.
Most people know their parents only as adults. All they
know about their parents' childhood are the verbal myths
parents pass along, usually at times of conflict between
parent and child. Father will say, "When I was a kid, we
used to have to walk five miles to school in snow up to
our waist, and you want to be driven two blocks in these
flurries!" Or, "When I was growing up, we were lucky to

get a new pair of shoes, but you're never satisfied unless you get the most expensive ones. I can remember walking in shoes with soles worn completely through. We would put a playing card inside them to keep our socks from wearing out on the cement."

Few people seem to know how their parents first met, how they felt as children growing up, whether their grandparents fought a lot or had a peaceful relationship, how love was expressed in that home, what the parents' aspirations were as teenagers—so much of the "stuff" that influenced later life for their parents, and even the values with which they raised their children. It becomes even more difficult to get any information on the childhood home life of our grandparents and great-grandparents. For most of us it is as if grandparents and great-grandparents lived only for a time to bear their children, then quickly vanished from the scene. They are phantoms whose looks we carry, whose names we carry, even, in fact, whose genetic coding we carry; but we know practically nothing about them.

Whether our family is in crisis or doing pretty well, it would be beneficial for us to do a little research into our family system. A good way to begin is by making what is called a flow chart: it is a graphic profile of our extended (intergenerational) family. On page 159 is a sample of how it will look.

Begin at the bottom of the page. Start with the newest generation in your family, then move up with each preceding generation. Use circles to indicate females, squares for males. Inside the circle/square indicate the person's age. For a deceased person, indicate the age at the time of death, mark a slash (/) on the circle/square, and state the year of death outside. Use a line to connect a husband and wife. For divorced people, draw two short lines across the connecting line. Keep the children on the side of the line with the parent with whom they lived. For unmarried couples living together, use a broken line.

When you are finished, you will end up with a very comprehensive view of how you are connected in life with your larger family. Make your chart as complete as you can. You will readily discover that there is much basic information you don't even know. Possibly missing are ages of nieces and nephews, years in which grandparents were married, years of the death of aunts or uncles. Try to find out that information.

Now, look at each member of the family and ask yourself, "How frequently do I see or speak to that person? What do I really know about him or her? How does his life affect me?" Look for patterns of similarity. Look also for patterns that seem to be opposed to yours.

I am not suggesting, nor should it be assumed by anyone, that we are always consciously balancing the ledger of our intergenerational family. The forces of indebtedness and shame within a family system run deep; the messages of need are communicated in subtle and often non-verbal ways from parent to child. They are even, at times, communicated to us when we are very young so that if we were asked why we did a particular thing, we might honestly answer, "It's just something I've always wanted to do." However, the reality is that there are reasons, and reasons within reasons, for our actions.

God created a universe of order. The rising and going down of the sun can be plotted and the time of these occurrences pinpointed each day. The tides of the sea are predictable. Lakes freeze from the top down. Each cell of each living thing carries its appropriate chemical combinations. Light behaves according to laws. Everything we experience is the way it is because it is conforming to some law of God.

The Bible tells us, "Honor your father and your mother, as the Lord your God has commanded you, so that you may live long and that it may go well with you in the land the Lord your God is giving you" (Deut. 5:16, NIV). This is a divine law for human behavior. We should not make the mistake of dismissing the emotional laws as nonsense. Like the physical laws, the emotional, or behavioral laws, work.

Two facets to the behavioral law to honor our parents need to be recognized. First, we are told that there is something life-producing about honoring our parents. The implication of "that your days may be long" is, in effect, "that you continue to live." Medical science has discovered that a direct relationship exists between our emotions and our health. It has long been known that ulcers, heart attack, and stroke are stress related, but we are finding today that cancer, skin diseases, and even the common cold develop more easily in a person in stress than in one at peace.

If, for one reason or another, you are living with a bitterness toward your mother or father, that bitterness could literally shorten your life. Always guarding, always hiding, a secret shame or guilt will wear you down and shorten your life in ways you might not even suspect.

The second facet to this law of God is in the words ". . . that it may go well with you in the land. . . ." This statement refers to your place within the society around you. Something about honoring your parents will establish well-being for you socially. Going back to our illustration of the Quincy family, we see how this part of the law might work.

Something caused great-grandfather Quincy, the one who went to prison for corruption in public office, to risk his career, his family, his very soul as it were, to enter into crime. Certainly, the nature of sin is within all of us, but some people we meet wouldn't steal, because stealing goes against something very strongly engrained within them. Some of these people are not at all religious and would simply reject stealing on the basis of its injustice to someone else.

Let us assume that great-grandfather Quincy lost his father when he was just a child. He, being the oldest child, felt the responsibility to help his mother provide money for the rest of the family. He quit school and began working full time (which years ago was not unusual for a teenager). As time went by he discovered that one of his skills was with people—communication. He didn't have the education to become a journalist, a college professor, or a director of public information, so he began to speak out loud on local issues for the political party that was strong in his neighborhood.

Slowly he began to see a career developing. He was feeling excited at the stirrings of power and financial security he had yearned for when he and his mother had been struggling to provide for the family. Of course, balanced against that security was the problem of compromise. At several points he found himself needing to compromise his feelings on issues with people stronger in the party if he wanted to continue his career. In American politics a candidate can win or lose overnight if certain powerful figures support or withdraw their support.

The position on the ladder of success became higher and higher and the small favors of the past became leverage for the big favors that were now being demanded. At this point his whole life was supported by the political system. He had enabled his family to be employed, which meant that if he went down, his relatives and their families would go down also. He had the proverbial tiger by the tail and was afraid of the consequences if he let go. He became an easy mark for large-scale political corruption.

The command to "honor your father and mother . . ." is not only a process of esteeming their value for yourself, but also of giving value back to them by the way you live. We fail to honor our parents if we bring disgrace on their name. Great-grandfather Quincy was honoring his parents by seeing the value of the family, affirming that value, and working to support the extended family. He dishonored his parents by blemishing the family name, and in an especially large way.

Great-grandfather Quincy's sons both worked at

honoring him. The country doctor honored him by
attempting to make up for his father's shame through
service to others—trading merit for shame. The son in
organized crime tried to honor his father by becoming a
family scapegoat and taking an even greater shame upon
himself. However, he, of course, dishonored his father
and mother, for this new shame added to the indebtedness
of the family to its society.

In the next generation of this family system, the issue of
shame arose again, and again on both sides. On one side,
another person entered organized crime; on the other,
someone became a heroin addict. In the same manner,
overgiving is seen on both sides, in the priest who gave up
being a natural father to be a father for society's children,
and in the politician who risked his life in the fight against
organized crime, a risk most people would not be willing
to take for him.

Of great help to this family system would be a fuller
understanding of the plight that led great-grandfather
on a course of increasing destructive momentum. This
suggestion is not meant to rationalize away wrong. Sin is
sin, and it comes with a price. However, there certainly are
biblical distinctions about the weight of responsibility and
the degree of punishment warranted in different situations.

Scripture deals with the sin of taking a man's life in three
categories of responsibility and punishment. The laws of
our land are fashioned after these distinctions. There is
premeditated murder, a planned killing. There is second
degree murder, a killing that is decided upon in the
emotion of a moment. Finally, there is manslaughter,
the taking of a life accidently by another, such as in an
automobile accident. Similarly, distinctions are made for
stealing. A man who steals a loaf of bread to feed his
family is not held as responsible as the person who steals
to enrich himself.

Of course, all of the acts cited above are sin. They miss
the perfect will of God for the way in which man should

live. Scripture tells us that we need to apply more grace to some acts of failure than to others, based on an understanding of the motives behind the act and the consequences to others. It is this grace that we as children need to attempt to work through in relation to the sins of our parents.

We have to come to the place where we can say, "My father made a bad decision; he did something really wrong, and he paid the price. But my father was not totally worthless. There was value to his life. He also did things that were good. And behind it all, I can see that he tried."

Too often we get caught up in looking at the pathology of our parents. Children in the church disavow their need to honor their parents because they claim their parents are not honorable. God's command never says they have to be honorable. It simply says that if we honor our parents, we will benefit; if we don't, we will lose.

If we measure carefully, we will find in the worst of mankind something of value. Isn't this idea the entire import of the gospel? Doesn't the Bible say, "For God so loved the world . . . "? Aren't we told that God's desire is that none should perish? Don't we believe as Christians that Jesus died for all mankind? If God can find in the most wicked person something worth redeeming, we as his children need simply to look a bit harder at our parents to find those areas of worth in their lives. For, if we cannot find ways to honor our earthly father and mother, we will have difficulty entering into an honorable relationship with God, who presents himself to us as our heavenly Parent.

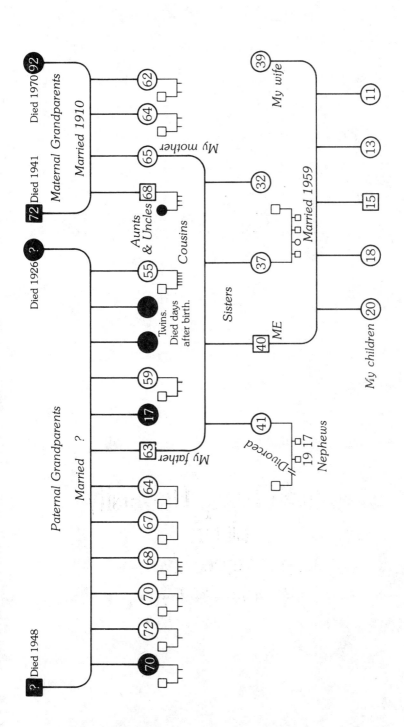